**The
Techniques of
Springboard
Diving**

The MIT Press
Massachusetts Institute of Technology
Cambridge, Massachusetts, and London, England

The Techniques of Springboard Diving

Charles Batterman

Copyright © 1968 by
The Massachusetts Institute of Technology

Set in Linofilm Helvetica.
Printed and bound in the United States of America
by Wm. J. Keller Inc.

Library of Congress catalog card number: 68-14457

Charlie Batterman is a true student of the analytical approach, and this book on diving reflects his approach to coaching—that of the scientist. He has studied mechanics and applied his knowledge to the field of coaching. Charlie not only understands *what* the diver should do for most efficient performance, he also knows *why* it should be done that way.

In 1956, I had the opportunity to be coached by Charlie Batterman. I was already a National Champion, and an Olympian, but in a few weekends I found out how *little* I really knew about diving. I had been coached by many people, but Charlie was the first one to stress the importance of the scientific approach. As a result of his efforts, I began analyzing my diving in terms of mechanical principles—for the first time figuring out the "why" of the sport. I am indebted to Charlie for his important contribution to my ultimate success as a competitive diver and as an inspiration toward my coaching career. [Bob won the Olympic Gold Medal in the summer of '56.]

This book is a must for all coaches and competitors who want to reach their full potential in diving.

Bob Clotworthy

Princeton University
March 1968

Acknowledgments

The most valuable help I received during the final draft of this book was from my daughter Amy, who organized and shaped the material into a logical and orderly sequence with a keen knowledge and instinct for simple understandable English. I did the drawings in this book myself because I wanted to be sure the figures were correctly positioned. My daughter Nora got me out of a a real dilemma by showing me how to indicate twist.

I am most grateful to all the divers and coaches who have indicated an interest in, and a desire to read, this book and particularly to the divers whose photographs appear in it: Bob Clotworthy, '56 Olympic Champion and Varsity Swimming Coach at Princeton; Lou Vitucci, Chuck Knorr, and Fletcher Gilders, who are fellow Ohio Staters and all National Intercollegiate and National A.A.U. Champions; Frank Manheim, Harvard '52; Holt Maness, Princeton '69; and Ken Sitzberger and Frank Gorman, Olympic Gold and Silver Medalists at the '64 Olympics in Tokyo. In addition, my thanks to Dr. Harold E. "Doc" Edgerton of M.I.T., whose great strobe shots illustrate many of the dives; and to his students, M.I.T. diver Dave Cahlander, who took many of the photographs, and Bruce DePalma, who developed the unique high-speed stroboscopic movie photography technique used in some of the sequences; and to my divers at Harvard and M.I.T. from whom I learned so much.

Charles Batterman

Cambridge, Massachusetts
January 1968

Contents

Almost without exception the published work on springboard diving has one failing. Divers and coaches write descriptions of dives based on what they *think* they see and feel rather than on logical explanations based on sound mechanics. Often things are not what they seem.

I remember meeting and talking with some European coaches who had successfully trained outstanding divers. They were adamant about certain principles. For example, they considered it an unwritten rule that a diver must *never* allow his hands and arms to move behind the center line of his body as he presses the board. They insisted that this (unnatural restriction) was what good divers did and that there was no other way, despite any explanation to the contrary. Indeed there was even skepticism after I pointed out that their own divers clearly disobeyed "the rule." The truth of the matter is that good divers instinctively do the natural and correct thing—despite coaching—and it is almost impossible properly to coordinate the arm movement with the press of the board *without* circling them back. As another example, it is a common belief that divers can leave the board with no forward lean whatsoever and be moved safely away by the flexibility of the diving board. Not so—but try to explain this to the traditionalists.

Speeding Up Learning Time

There is no doubt that teaching with traditional ideas and methods can eventually be successful. However, specific understanding of what makes dives happen, and why, can be a great aid to a coach. Through his knowledge of mechanics and fundamentals he can shorten the time needed to improve his pupil's performance. How many times have we seen a young diver make mistake after mistake, only eventually achieving some degree of success through the painful process of trial and error. A word from an informed instructor could have brought the diver success in a fraction of the time.

A good understanding of diving mechanics can make a good coach a better one. He can become a keen analyst and trouble shooter and avoid relying on often inaccurate traditional ideas and the devious route of trial and error.

Improvement in Diving

Diving has been progressing rapidly. The unification of the rules through the concerted effort of the Amateur Athletic Union (A.A.U.) and the National Collegiate Athletic Association (N.C.A.A.) and the Federación Internacional de Natación (F.I.N.A.) have standardized requirements, the equipment, and consequently, training. In recent years there has been such improvement in the construction and materials of diving boards that dives previously considered impossible are commonplace today. In a recent National A.A.U. championship *all* the eight finalists did a three-and-a-half somersault. Most of them performed reverse and back two-and-a-half somersaults and reverse and back two-and-a-half twisting one-and-a-half somersaults. The inward two-and-a-half has become a necessary dive in national and international competition. With more efficient apparatus, there is a

growing awareness among diving coaches of the mechanics of the use of the board and the forces that initiate and control the movement of the body in space. The result will be a more effective coaching style. The search for better understanding and new training methods is a healthy sign for the growth of diving.

Keep an open mind—don't be intimidated. None of the following material is too difficult if the coach or student keeps an open mind. Understanding a few basic rules makes it much easier to correct errors of technique. For example, if a diver is having difficulty completing a forward two-and-a-half somersault, all the pleading in the world for him to spin faster will not help unless he can be given *specific* directions: "Bring your arms and head down sooner and faster—*before* your feet leave the board."

The first chapter attempts to explain in simple terms some of the laws of motion that govern and control the diving movements. *Read them.* Understand the terms and then go on to read the general principles and the descriptions of the dives. Cause and effect is what you're after. What makes specific things happen in a dive? Understanding the whys and hows makes both learning and coaching much simpler.

Newton's Third Law of Motion

A good understanding of diving mechanics requires a good understanding of Newton's "third law." A great deal of what happens in the air, and indeed before the diver leaves the board, depends on it. The law states that for every action there is an equal and opposite reaction. This means that when a force is applied in one direction against an object, the object returns the force equally and in the opposite direction. (1.1)

When a rocket thrusts hot gases back, the gases push back against the rocket equally and in the opposite direction, resulting in a lifting movement. When a swimmer pushes back against the water, the water pushes back against the swimmer's arm, moving him ahead. A diver who pushes down against the surface of the diving board is being pushed up by the board; if he pushes backward, the board pushes forward against his feet (see Chapter 11); if he pushes sideways, the board pushes back the other way. This is how both twist and spin are started from the board.

1.1
At the start of a race a swimmer pushes *back* against the wall, which in turn pushes his body forward for the dive.

A Body Free in Space: After a diver is in the air, if he moves one part of his body in one direction, the rest of his body reacts by moving in the opposite direction. Should he move his arms to the right across his chest, his body will twist to the left and not to the right, as commonly believed. (1.2) From a pike position, if he moves his legs out of the pike, his upper body will move away from the legs, and his legs will move away from the body as well. (1.3)

Center of Gravity

The center of gravity is an imaginary point around which the body weight is equally distributed. In spinning dives a diver always spins around his center of gravity. It can fall outside of the body proper. When a diver bends over into a pike position, his center of gravity can be somewhere in the space between his upper body and his legs. (1.4)

Center of gravity is really the point around which the body is in equilibrium.

Linear and Angular Motion

Linear motion refers to movement in a straight line. A train moving along a straight track exhibits linear motion. When it goes around a curve, it has angular motion. When a diver spins in a one-and-a-half somersault or twists in a double twister, he exhibits angular motion.

Angular Velocity

Angular velocity refers to the speed of the spin, the revolutions per minute. The angular velocity of a spinning body may be changed because it depends on the moment of inertia.

Moment of Inertia

Moment of inertia is a property of bodies having rotational motion around an axis. It is the mass times the square of the distance of the center of that mass to the axis of rotation. This distance is referred to as the *radius of gyration*. Because the mass (or weight) of the various body parts remains constant in diving, the significant factor in determining speed of the spin is the radius of gyration. When a diver tucks his body into a ball, he shortens the radius of gyration, and the moment of inertia decreases. This speeds up the spin.

Angular Momentum

For our purposes angular momentum may be referred to as the *amount* of spin and is expressed as the moment of inertia multiplied by the angular velocity. It is not the same as the speed of the spin.

If a diver turns as he leaves the board, he has angular momentum. He cannot get it once he is in the air. The *amount* of spin must be determined from the diving board.

1.2
Moving the arm across the chest to the left will twist the body to the right.

1.3
When a pike position is opened in the air, the legs move away from the arms, and the arms move away from the legs.

1.4
The center of gravity doesn't always fall within the body.

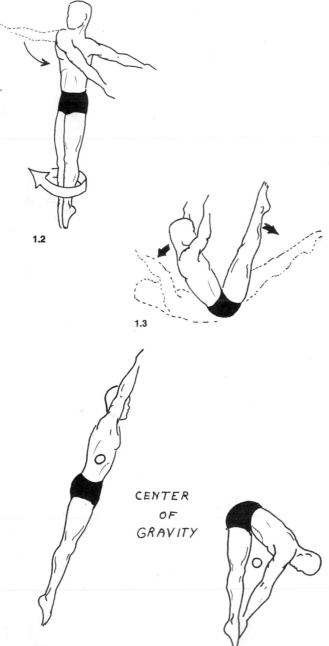

1.2

1.3

CENTER
OF
GRAVITY

1.4

Conservation of Angular Momentum

Aside from the introduction of outside forces, the angular momentum of a body is conserved. It is constant. This means that once he is spinning and has left the board, a diver will continue to have the *same* angular momentum until he hits the water. (Air resistance is negligible.)

When a diver tucks (thereby shortening the radius of gyration), then according to the law of conservation of angular momentum the spin must speed up. Remember: the moment of inertia times the angular velocity (the speed of the spin) equals the angular momentum. If one value is decreased, then the other must increase to conserve the angular momentum (the spin speeds up). When the diver moves his weight away from the spinning axis, the moment of inertia increases, and the spin slows down to conserve the angular momentum.

Inertia

Inertia refers to the tendency of a body's momentum to remain constant, when at rest to remain at rest, or when in motion in a straight line to remain in motion unless acted on by outside forces. For example, if a car is suddenly braked to a stop, the people sitting in the car lurch forward. Since they had momentum forward when the car stopped, they continue forward because of inertia. The friction of their bodies against the seat stops them— sometimes. A diver moves forward during his hurdle. When he lands on the end of the board, the body continues to move forward as the feet are stopped by friction. A forward lean results even if the diver lands on the end of the board vertically. (See Chapter 2.)

Friction

Friction is the resistance objects have to being pushed or dragged across one another. When two flat surfaces are put together, friction makes it difficult to pull one along the other. Friction is what enables a diver to walk on the board and to land on the end without sliding off. The rougher the surface, the greater the friction. (This is why board surfaces are embedded with nonskid material.)

Centrifugal Force

Centrifugal force pulls a moving body outward when it is moving in a circular path. The classic representation of this is a bucket of water swung in a circle; the water doesn't pour out of the bucket when it is upside down because of the centrifugal force of the water against the bottom of the bucket.

Torque

Torque is a force or combination of forces that tends to produce a rotating or twisting motion about an axis. In diving, a torque must be introduced for twist or spin to occur. In a half twist layout, the torque is usually introduced by pushing the feet sideways as well as forward against the board as it lifts. (1.5)

1.5
Introducing the torque for a half twist from the board.

6   The Body Axes

An axis is an imaginary axle around which a body rotates. When a diver spins or twists, he always turns around an axis. The center of gravity of the body *always* falls within the spinning axis.

There are an infinite number of axes around which a body may rotate, but for the purposes of diving there are three. (1.6)

The Transverse or Lateral Spinning Axis: This side-to-side axis is the one around which the body rotates when doing a forward, backward, inward, or reverse spinning dive.

The Dorsoventral Axis: This is the front-to-back axis, an imaginary pole entering the chest and going out the back. The body turns somewhat on this axis when a twister is started from a pike or layout spinning dive. The body in these dives turns sideways, as in a cart-wheel, around the dorsoventral axis.

The Vertical or Long Body Axis: This is the up-and-down axis, the one from the head to the feet. Whenever the body twists in a dive, the body is turning on the long or vertical axis.

In a full twisting one-and-a-half somersault, for example, the body will be turning around all three at some time in the dive: the lateral when it spins forward, the dorsoventral when the arms are circled and the body tipped off the forward spinning axis, and around the vertical body axis during the twist.

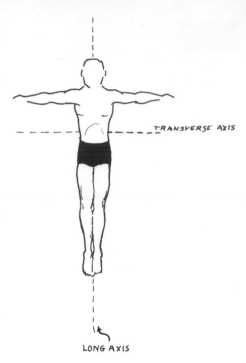

The Path of a Projected Body

When a body is projected at an angle upward (as in a hurdle or a dive), the center of gravity of the body moves in a parabolic path with the horizontal velocity remaining constant.

This path of the center of gravity will be unalterable, regardless of the changes in the shape of the body itself, without the introduction of an outside force. For example, when a diver leaves the board for any dive, whether he spins into a two-and-a-half somersault, twists, goes forward or reverse, the path of the center of gravity remains unalterably the parabolic one described. However, the body position and the distribution of its mass around the center of gravity may change. When this occurs while a person is standing on the ground, as when he moves his arms and/or leg up and down, the center of gravity moves up and down within the body.

When this happens in the air, the distribution of the body mass around the center of gravity changes because the center of gravity *must* stay in the projected path. For example, in the air during a hurdle when the lifted knee moves down, the body moves up because the center of gravity must stay in its parabolic path (and the position of the center of gravity is changed within the body).

For good boardwork this is an important principle to understand, as it determines the type of hurdle that is desirable for a particular dive. (See Chapter 2.)

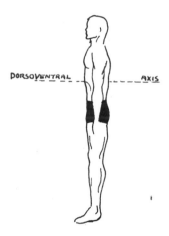

1.6
The body axes.

¹The terms mass and weight can be interchanged as far as diving is concerned because the pull of gravity is constant.

Using the diving board properly is a major problem for coaches and pupils because *most of what happens during a dive is determined* BEFORE *the diver leaves the board*. The flight of the dive, the lift, the distance from the board, the amount and direction of the spin are all determined *before* the diver is in the air. Obviously, without good boardwork a diver works at a great handicap because what he is able to do in the air is determined, controlled, and also *limited* by what he does on the board, on both forward and backward takeoffs.

The Natural Manner

Whenever possible, a diver should adopt a natural style in his boardwork. All movements should be similar to those he performs naturally every day such as walking, running, and jumping. (2.1)

A diver *walks* for the first two steps of the approach, heel and toe, exactly as he walks down the street. (2.2) The third step of the approach is similar to a *running* (or hopping) step. The hurdle and the third step are not separate; the hurdle begins *as* the foot is placed for the third step.

When leaving the board, either forward or backward, the position of the body and the movements of the arms are the same as those in an *ordinary jump upward*.

In the air, a diver should avoid exaggerated body positions such as excessive arch or abnormal head positions. Try to be graceful and natural.

2
The Forward Approach

2.1
The forward approach, clearly illustrating that the arms circle *up* as the board is pushed down.

Photographic sequences run horizontally throughout the book.

2.2   a   b   c   d   e   f   g   h

2.3

Seeing the End of the Board

A minimum of three steps plus the hurdle are required, and from the beginning the diver's eyes should be focused on the end of the board. *He should always see his feet land.*

During the entire approach, the body is *erect, well balanced,* and the hurdle is *long*—approximately the length of a normal three-foot step.

Position of the Fulcrum and the Starting Point

The starting point for the approach is easily determined by executing the approach from the diving end of the board toward the fulcrum and marking that point. A diver should always start from the same spot.

If the diving board has an adjustable fulcrum, then the position of the fulcrum should be determined by trial and error (according to personal preference) in practice approaches. It is wise in practice to do an approach, hurdle, and one bounce only. Excessive and repeated bouncing of the board is dangerous and not too beneficial.

Now let's consider the parts separately.

The Address

The diver stands at attention at his starting point for several seconds to prepare himself for the dive and to give the judges an opportunity to focus their attention on him. This should be done for no more than three to five seconds. Be a showman.

First and Second Steps

As previously mentioned, these are natural walking steps, heel and toe, with the eyes focused on the target—the end of the board. The arms hang at the sides and swing naturally.

The body is erect, well balanced, and the steps *even* or progressively increasing in length.

It is very important that the *rhythm remain constant.* Errors of balance and rhythm (such as leaning forward excessively on the second step or hurrying over it) will have an adverse effect on the hurdle and takeoff.

2.2
The forward approach, including hurdle. The natural manner.

2.3
Press down and *back* with the takeoff leg for a long hurdle.

Third Step and Takeoff into the Hurdle

These two parts of the approach must be considered together because the placing of the third step and the beginning of the hurdle *happen at the same time.*

A good diver is lifted into the hurdle by the action of the board, not by jumping up himself. Consequently, the placing of the third step is critical because every movement the diver makes at this point should help push the board down: (1) he moves his body from the erect position quickly downward; (2) he lifts his arms diagonally forward and upward; (3) he lifts one knee. (See 2.2d.) All three of these movements occur at *exactly* the same instant and work in the following manner.

As the knee flexes, the body weight moves down, and the momentum starts depressing the board. At the same time the lifting of the arms and the other knee increase the downward force because, according to Newton's third law, the reaction to these lifting movements is a downward press of the body against the board. Clearly, the arms and knee lift in order to push the board down farther, not to jump up. The recoil of the depressed board throws the diver into the air for a high hurdle. To convince yourself of this, study movies of good divers. You will see that the arms and knee are already lifted when the board is fully depressed. (See 2.2d.)

Picture the position of the diver at this moment: the board is fully depressed, and he is standing on one leg, knee slightly bent, with the arms and the other knee lifted. When the depressed board begins to rise, the diver extends the takeoff leg (the one he's standing on), pointing the toe fully to push against the lifting board. He also pushes slightly backward in order to move the body forward, i.e., to get a long hurdle. (2.3)

The Hurdle

The hurdle should be the length of a normal step and should move forward with the *same momentum* established in the first two steps.

The Value of a Long Hurdle: In *all* dives from a springboard, there *must* be some forward lean to move the diver out far enough to avoid hitting the board.[1] With a long hurdle the diver has considerable forward momentum so that after the feet land and are stopped by friction, the body continues to move forward. Due to inertia the momentum remains constant, and a diver correctly feels that he lands on the end of the board *with no lean.* The lean develops *after* the feet land, during the time the board moves down and up.

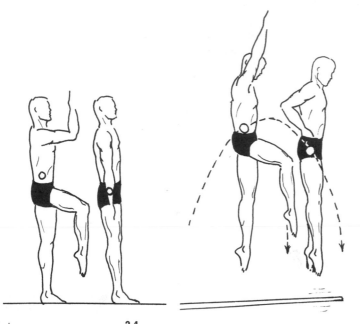

2.4
The center of gravity can move up and down in the body but must stay in its parabolic path in the air.

2.5
The arms, head, and body move down *before* the feet leave the board for a two-and-a-half pike from the one-meter board. (Diver is Olympic and National Champion, Lou Vitucci.)

Lowering the Lifted Knee on the Way Up: The diver leaves the board and goes into the hurdle as described, and the lifted knee begins to straighten on the way up so that at the peak of the hurdle lift both legs are straight.

We know that once a body is free in space, the center of gravity *must* move in a predetermined parabolic path. We also know that the diver had one knee lifted and the other straight at the moment he left the board. When the lifted leg is lowered on the way up, the center of gravity moves down in the body. (2.4) Since the trajectory of the center of gravity cannot change, the body must move up when the leg is lowered. This gives the diver the feeling that he stays in the air a longer time, and in fact he does. The added time in the air better prepares him for the landing on the end of the board.

During the drop to the end of the board, the head is rotated down, eyes looking over the chest at the end of the board. The body is straight (no pike or arch), and the diver falls to the end of the board, landing on the balls of the feet. As he falls, the arms begin to *circle* back, down, and around. It is commonly believed that circling the arms back is bad whereas just the contrary is true. Never restrict the natural circling of the arms. When the arms finally circle up, there is a reaction causing a downward force that is transmitted to the board. (Note in 2.2f that the arms are well above the shoulders when the board is at its maximum depression.)

Takeoff into the Dive

As the board begins to rise, the arms continue to reach, and the diver "rides" the lifting board, extending the legs and pointing the toes. With the final lift of the board, the arms continue to reach up in reverse dives or begin to move down in forward spinning dives *before the feet leave the board.* (2.5)

Forward Lean on the Takeoff: The angle of takeoff for dives varies. In all cases, however, there must be at least a slight forward lean. If there were none, the diver would hit the board.

In forward spinning dives there is more lean than in the reverse group. The reason for this will be explained in Chapter 5.

Points To Remember

1. Stand at attention for about three seconds before starting.

2. Walk naturally.

3. Use a hurdle about as long as a normal walking step—for an adult usually about three feet. This keeps forward momentum constant.

4. Lift the arms and knee *as the foot is placed* for the third step—not afterward.

5. Lower the knee on the way up in the hurdle.

6. *Watch the end of the board—always* See your feet land.

7. Keep the rhythm of the approach even.

[1]A long hurdle refers to one that is approximately the length of a normal stride—about 3 to 4 feet for an adult.
Theoretically if a diver moves forward fast enough during his hurdle, he can safely take off into a dive with no forward lean at all. The resultant of the two forces, his forward momentum and the lifting force of the board, would move him diagonally forward and up. Only with excessive forward speed in the hurdle would this be possible. The natural and rather slow walking style of the approach used in springboard diving makes some forward lean essential for all takeoffs.

Contrary to what is popularly supposed to be true, the backward takeoff is *not* the same for every dive. Variations occur as the board is lifting (as the diver "rides" the lifting board) depending on the dive to be done and the direction of the spin.

Since we know that spin direction is determined before the diver is in the air, clearly certain things must be done to spin inward and different things done to spin backward.

The Back Takeoff

As in the front takeoff, the diver assumes an attention position at his starting point and stands there for no more than three seconds. He then walks briskly to the end of the board, turns around, and stands backward. No particular way of turning is necessary because the dive doesn't officially begin until the position at the end of the board is maintained and the arms lowered.

Balancing on the End of the Board: The body is straight (no arch ever) and the head up with the eyes focused on the other end of the board. The arms are raised to shoulder level, shoulder width apart, fingers straight and together. Then the feet are placed one at a time, with about half the foot extending back over the end of the board. (3.1)

The feet are in a triangular position, toes about one inch apart and heels together, making a tripod base with the heels slightly higher than the end of the board. This position is maintained for a few seconds, and then the arms are slowly lowered to the sides. There should be a slight pause here to allow for the

14

3.1
The back takeoff. The arms *lift* as the board is pushed down.

c

f

i

l

adjustment of balance necessary because of the shifting of the center of gravity when the arms are lowered.

The Press of the Board: The procedure for depressing the board begins with a lowering of the heels, which moves the body weight down. As the board is depressed by the downward momentum of the body, the arms are brought up sideways, *neither forward nor back* (to prevent changes in the body balance), to a point at least as high as shoulder level or slightly higher. Then when the board rises, the heels are raised above the level of the board so that the diver is standing on his toes, arms up and out to the sides, when the board has rebounded to its highest.

The arms then begin to circle back, down, and around, and the body weight is moved down by sitting back. This action pushes the board down while the arms continue their circular movement *up* in front of the body as the board moves down.

With the board fully depressed, the diver is in a sitting position with the arms at or above shoulder level. (Note in 3.1 that the board is fully depressed and the arms are *already up*.) As the board recoils and lifts, the diver "rides" it, extending the legs and toes and pushing sharply against the lifting board.

The Takeoff into the Dive: Depending on the dive to be done, the arms either continue to move up for a back spinning dive or change direction and move down for inward dives during the final lift of the board. (See Chapter 14.)

Starting the Board Moving: At the start of the press the heels are lowered and then the arms lifted side-up to increase the push down against the moving board (Newton's third law). This is good because it gives the diver a "live" board to work from. Once the board has been moved in this manner (by the lowering of the heels), all the subsequent movements of the body and arms must occur in a sequence to match and increase the up-and-down movement of the board. The farther down the board can be pressed, the greater the lifting force when it recoils up and the longer time that force is applied to the body, resulting in maximum lift.

The Action of the Board for a Back Takeoff:
After the initial downward movement of the board, it moves up, way down, and then up again as it throws the diver into the air.

The arms help to push the board down. During the second time down, the body weight is lowered by flexing the knees and hips. At the same time the arms are circled around and *up*. It is essential that the *arms are lifted when the board is being pushed down,* NOT *when the board is lifting!* This is a difficult concept— but the arm lift is necessary to increase the downward force against the board. To prove this, stand on a spring scale with your arms down at your sides. Bring your arms quickly side-up to shoulder level. The scale will register about forty pounds of additional weight. Conversely, start with the arms horizontally out to the sides and bring them quickly down to your sides. A comparable weight decrease will be noted.

Establishing Backward Lean: A diver must move his weight back for all back takeoff dives, or he will hit the board. (3.2) For inward dives, by sitting back, i.e., moving the hips back rather than the shoulders and head, the diver can (1) get the necessary lean; (2) be in a good position for starting inward spin; and (3) still be in the natural position for jumping up. The amount of lean must be greater for back spinning dives than for inward spinning ones. This is due to the push of the feet forward for inward dives (which moves the body away from the board) and backward for back dives (which tends to move the body toward the board). (This will be explained in detail in Chapters 8 and 14.)

The Final Lift: As you read on, it will become clear that all spins must start from the board. Therefore, what happens when the diver is in final contact with the lifting board is very important. Either inward or backward spin has to be established at this moment. One can neither start nor control the direction of a sustained spin after having left the board.

Points To Remember

1. Do not delay before taking your position. The dive doesn't start until you are at the end of the board.

2. Always pause after the arms are lowered to adjust your balance.

3. To start, lower the heel and bring the arms directly side-up. Avoid forward or backward movement of the arms.

4. Always sit the hips back and *lift* the arms as the board is pushed down.

5. Start your spin before you are in the air.

3.2
Moving the hips back as the board is pressed, as shown by '64 Olympic Champion, Ken Sitzberger.

3.2

There are three body positions divers can use: tuck, pike, or layout. Many of the listed dives can be done in any of the three positions, plus the combinations known as flying position and free position.

Tuck

In the tuck position the diver is in a tight ball, his knees and hips fully flexed, hands grasping the shins just under the knees, and the knees pulled close to the chest. For forward and inward spins the head is down with the eyes looking over the feet. (4.1)

For back and reverse spins the head is usually up, in line with the body.

The Spread-Knee Tuck Position: The tighter the tuck, the faster the spin. For this reason many divers now use a tuck position in which the knees are spread slightly and the head pulled down between the knees. This is acceptable and provides the fastest possible spin because the weight is closest to the axis of rotation. (Angular momentum is conserved —the shortening of the radius of gyration results in an increase in the velocity of the spin.) (4.2)

4.1
The proper tuck position for (a) forward and inward spins, and (b) back and reverse spins.
4.2
The spread-knee tuck position speeds up the spin.

4.1

4.2

Pike

When using the pike position, the diver is bent at the waist with the legs straight. There are three acceptable ways of doing a pike dive:

1. *Open Pike:* The arms are extended sideways at right angles to the body. (4.3) This is a very attractive style, but its use is limited to one-and-a-half somersaults because it is difficult to overcome the centrifugal pull that tends to open the pike during the spin. The diver must keep the hip flexors (the abdominal and quadriceps muscles) tightly contracted to counteract this. For more than one-and-a-half somersaults, the pike position usually is closed.

2. *Closed Pike:* The body is again bent at the waist with the legs straight, and the arms grasp the legs just behind the knees. The upper body is pulled close to the thighs. For forward and inward spins, the head is down but positioned so that the diver is able to see over his legs. (4.4) For backward and reverse spinning dives the head is slightly raised to align with the upper body.

3. *The "Jackknife" Position:* The jackknife position is used only in the required dives. The hands touch the toes, the knees are straight, and the pike is tight. (4.5)

4.3
The proper open-pike position.
4.4
A forward one-and-a-half, illustrating a perfect closed pike.
4.5
The jackknife position which is used only for half somersault dives.

4.3

4.4

4.5

Layout

The layout position is rarely used for forward spinning dives other than the front dive. In a proper layout the body is straight or slightly arched, and the arms are out to the sides at right angles to the body, as in a swan dive (4.6), or down at the sides, as in a back one-and-a-half layout. (4.7)

Flying Somersaults

The category known as flying dives starts with the body turning in the layout position until the diver has completed half a turn (the legs must be vertical). Then the body is brought quickly to a tuck or pike position in which the diver finishes the required number of turns. For example, in a flying one-and-a-half somersault tuck, the diver would start in "swan" position until the legs were vertically up, followed by a tuck for the rest of the spin to a head-first entry.

Free Position

The free position is a recent adaptation for multiple spinning-twisting dives (double twisting one-and-a-half) where the diver starts in a pike position, twists in the layout position, and then finishes the dive in pike position again.

4.6
The correct layout position as seen in a front dive.
4.7
The correct layout position of a back one-and-a-half somersault layout.

4.6

4.7

To understand the mechanics of the forward spinning dives, several preliminary concepts are necessary.

1. There *must be some forward lean* for *all* forward spinning dives.

2. The spin *must start from the board* and cannot be started after the diver is in the air.

3. There must be more forward lean than is needed for the group of reverse dives.

Moving the Weight Forward; Leaning

Lean moves a diver safely away from the diving board and also helps start forward spin. As was fully explained in Chapter 2, the style of approach that uses a long hurdle (about three feet for adults) results in sufficient forward lean to take care of the requirements of the dive, even if the body is vertical as it lands on the end of the board. For this reason a diver *correctly* feels that he lands on the board with no lean forward. The momentum of his hurdle results in forward lean which is *essential* for all forward spinning dives. (5.1)

Starting the Forward Spin

Just deciding to spin isn't going to do it. Specific directions are needed. What starts the diver turning? Obviously something different must be done to spin forward than to start a reverse spinning dive.

The Push of the Feet: The answer lies primarily in an understanding of the often-mentioned Newtonian law, the Third Law of Motion. Before a diver leaves the board for a forward spinning dive, *his feet must push forward* against the surface of the board—toward the tip of the board. (5.1d) By applying the principle of the third law, the diving board will push back against the feet equally and in the opposite direction. When combined with the necessary slight forward lean, it starts the body rotating forward. Whether consciously or not, *the diver does this on all forward spinning dives*.

Another way to get spin would be to have a considerable amount of forward lean as the diving board lifts. However, this is a poor technique because it results in a dive that goes far out with little lift.

In addition to starting spin, pushing the feet forward moves the body in the opposite direction—in this case, toward the back end of the diving board. Therefore, it is essential to have some forward lean for all forward spinning dives, more than would be required for reverse dives. In reverse dives the push *back* on the takeoff moves the body away from the board and starts the reverse spin as well.

5.1
The forward momentum of a moving hurdle results in a slight forward lean. The feet push *forward* (heavy arrow) to start the body spinning forward.

5.1

a   b   c   d

Starting the Spin from the Board: *Once the diver's feet have left the board, he has all the spin he will ever have.* Therefore if a great deal of forward spin is required (as for a two-and-a-half somersault, pike position, from the one-meter board), the head, arms, and upper torso must be moving down rapidly as the board lifts, not afterward. (5.2) This is important for two reasons.

1. To transfer spin from the upper body: after the torso moves down, there is a transfer of angular momentum to the entire body when it goes into the air, contributing to the spinning force.

2. To avoid "getting stuck" in the dive: if the head and arms are brought down in the air, the legs will lift to counteract this movement (Newton's third law again). The result will be "drawing the legs" or, in other words, not enough spin. Clearly, for all forward spinning dives the upper body must be moving down *before* the feet leave the board, not afterward. The speed and extent to which this is done will vary with the spin requirements of the dive.

5.2
Start of a two-and-a-half somersault pike from the one-meter board. Notice how far the upper body moves down before the feet leave the board when lots of spin is needed. (Lou Vitucci is the diver.)

5.3
Decreasing the radius of gyration speeds up the spin.

5.2

Speeding Up and Slowing Down the Spin in the Air

There are two concepts related to spinning in a dive: one refers to the *amount* of spin and the other to the *speed* of the spin. Technically, the amount of spin (the initial spin) is the angular momentum. The speed of the spin, the revolutions per minute, is the angular velocity. These terms have been explained in Chapter 1. Briefly, the difference between the two is that angular momentum is a constant, whereas angular velocity can change when the body position changes.[1] (5.3)

The Entry

Since angular momentum is conserved, the forward spin can never be completely stopped. It can only be slowed down. When the legs and arms are fully extended, as during an entry into the water head first, the spin will be at its slowest for a given dive since the weight will be farthest from the axis of rotation. But there *will* be some spin left. Therefore, the angle of entry for all forward spinning dives should be slightly short of vertical.

[1]Actually, the velocity of the spin is controlled by increasing or decreasing the moment of inertia around the spinning axis. (5.3) According to the Law of Conservation of Angular Momentum, when the moment of inertia increases, the spin slows down, and vice versa.
Since moment of inertia is equal to the mass times the square of the distance of that mass from the axis of rotation, then the farther away from the axis the mass (weight) is, the slower the spin for a given angular momentum. (The following results are proportionally correct although, to simplify, the factor of the pull of gravity which is constant is ignored, and weight is substituted for mass.)
The formula for moment of inertia is $I = mr^2$.
 I = moment of inertia
 m = the mass (weight)
 r = the radius (the distance between the mass and the axis of rotation)
Assume that a person's legs weigh 50 pounds and the center of gravity of the legs is 20 inches from the spinning axis when the legs are straight.
Since $m = 50$ pounds and $r = 20$ inches,
then $mr^2 = 50 \times 20^2$ and
 $I = 20,000$.
If the legs are drawn into a tuck position and their center of gravity is then 5 inches from the spinning axis, then $m = 50$, $r = 5$, $mr^2 = 50 \times 5^2$, and
 $I = 1250$.
This means that when the legs are tucked, they will want to spin 16 times faster than when they are straight.

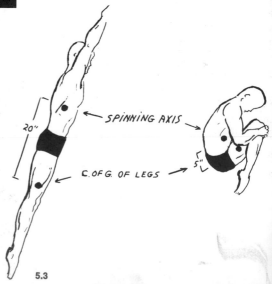

20"

← SPINNING AXIS →

C. OF G. OF LEGS →

5"

5.3

Front Dive Layout ("Swan" Dive)

The swan dive is considered a most beautiful dive. Its exacting technique makes it a difficult dive to do well, but for the spectator it is simple and beautiful.

Directions to the Diver

As the board lifts, reach up; lift the head and chest while pushing down and *forward* with the feet. Quickly place the arms straight out to the sides, arch slightly (chest arch), look straight ahead, and hold this position. (6.1) When the legs have lifted, easily bring the hands together and stretch for the entry, eliminating any arch. Look at the water over the tops of the hands and take the dive straight down.

Mechanics of the Dive

In most forward spinning dives the head and arms are lowered to help start the spin from the board. The rules governing the swan dive demand that the head be lifted and the arms placed to the sides. Therefore, to introduce forward spin while lifting the upper body to swan position, the emphasis *must* be on a sharp forward push against the board during the takeoff.

Controlling the Dive in the Air: Since the layout position must be maintained in the swan dive, it is difficult to increase the speed of the spin in the air. A very accurate amount of forward spin must be initiated *from* the board. There is, however, one acceptable thing that can be done. By increasing the body arch, the diver can speed up his spin just as he does when the body bends in the opposite direction, as in a jackknife. Despite the fact that the body bends in opposite directions, the results of piking or arching are the same: the weight moves closer to the spinning axis, and the spin speeds up. Under no circumstances should the head be lowered, as this spoils the appearance of the dive and does little if anything to help. If too much spin has developed, the arch can be eliminated early and the arms extended forward to slow down the spin.

The Stretch for the Entry: The entry is made slightly short of vertical to allow for the small amount of spin that remains after the body is stretched straight.

Points To Remember

1. Use a very slight forward lean.

2. Lift the arms, head, and chest, and push *forward* with the feet as the board lifts.

3. Take the swan position immediately. Don't wait.

4. Increase the arch if you haven't enough spin and lengthen out (no arch and arms extended overhead) if there's too much spin.

5. Stretch for the entry and take the dive down.

6.1
Swan dive; correct position in the air and proper alignment for the entry of a front dive layout.

6.2
Jackknife; good position, but dive is too far out.

Front Dive Pike ("Jackknife")

In competition the required front dive may be done either in layout or pike position. Of the two the swan dive is more difficult to do well. If the front dive is piked, the pike position can be held for as long or short a time as needed to control the dive for a good entry. This will be explained fully.

Directions to the Diver

After seeing your feet land on the end of the board, watch the entry point on the water surface—*never lift the head*. Take the dive up with the head and arms moving easily down. Move the hips above the head and touch the toes in a tight pike. Keep looking at the water. Open the pike and move the arms *forward* to line up for the entry. (6.2)

Mechanics of the Dive

A jackknife must start from the board. If you bend over after you're in the air, the legs will move forward. Consequently the touch will be made well forward of vertical, and the diver will be "stuck"—not enough spin.

Completing the Dive on the Way Up: Once the diver's feet have left the board, the angular momentum, the lift, and the distance are all determined. At what point in the dive the pike is taken will not seriously affect the dive. Therefore, piking early, on the way up, results in a dive that is finished early and has a long drop to the water—a pleasing style.

Controlling the Spin for the Entry: The diver uses the length of time he stays in the pike as a check; it is a means of controlling the speed of his spin. He holds the pike for as long or as short a time as required to put the upper body in the correct entry position. When he reaches this position, he is ready to stretch for the entry, but his arms are pointing in the wrong direction—under him. To correct this, the arms *must move forward* to line up properly.

Points To Remember

1. See your feet land. Don't lift the head on the takeoff.

2. Use a round-shouldered lift of the back.

3. Watch the water from start to finish.

4. Start the dive from the board by lowering the head and lifting the hips easily.

5. Move the arms forward to line up the entry.

6. Play the dive slightly short of vertical—take it down.

The forward spinning group of dives includes all those in which the body turns forward (on the lateral spinning axis), from the front dive to the three-and-one-half somersault.

High or Low Board

No differentiation has been made for dives to be done from the one- or three-meter boards. In most cases the technique is the same. There are, however, some dives that lend themselves particularly to one or the other. A three-and-one-half somersault is successful only from the three-meter board. A two-and-one-half somersault pike works well for either board. A one-and-one-half somersault tuck is invariably used only from the one-meter board.

Technique for All Forward Spins

Generally, the technique used to spin forward for one, or four, somersaults is the same. The difference is one of degree. Clearly, more angular momentum (initial spin) must be established from the board to do a three-and-one-half somersault than would be needed for one somersault. The *method* of spinning is the same. The *amount* of spin started from the board is the difference.

It is agreed that under ordinary circumstances the forward lean is constant for all forward spinning dives. There must be some, but it should be minimal and not vary considerably.

Varying the Downward Movement of the Body:

The distance and the speed with which the arms and upper body are brought down as the board lifts will definitely affect the angular momentum (spin) started from the board. (See Chapter 5, Forward Spinning Dives: General Principles.)

A diver will bring the upper body down faster and farther and push forward harder with the feet as the number of somersaults increases.

Forward One-and-a-Half Somersault Tuck

Directions to the Diver

As the board lifts, extend the legs, move the head and arms easily down, and lift the upper back and hips. (7.1) Bring the head down under the lifting hips and squeeze into a tight tuck. After one somersault *see* the water and then kick the legs out and up, moving the arms *forward* and down to line up the entry. Enter slightly short of vertical.

Points To Remember

1. *Not much spin is needed.* Since a small amount of spin is needed in this dive, it is advantageous to get maximum lift by lifting the back in a round-shouldered manner and moving only the head and arms down.

2. Always look for the water before the entry.

Forward Double Somersault Tuck

Directions to the Diver

As soon as the feet leave the board, move *immediately* into a tight tuck position.

Since it is impossible to see the water to judge the entry (if you do, it's too late), you must—through practice—learn to use as gauges the speed of the spin, the amount of time you have been spinning, and a general "feel" to determine when to open for the entry.

Kick the legs out slightly short, sliding the hands to the sides. Then by increasing the arch as much as is needed, align the body for the proper entry. (7.2)

Points To Remember

1. *Never* lift the head during the takeoff; try to spin on the way up.

2. Always play the entry short. It is simple to adjust the entry by increasing the body arch as in the illustration. If the dive is over, it's a tough situation. There is almost nothing you can do.

Forward Two-and-a-Half Somersault Tuck

Directions to the Diver

Start the spin before the feet leave the board and move *immediately* into a tight tuck position, pulling the legs close to the chest. (Never lift the head on the takeoff.) The tighter the tuck, the faster the spin.

Look for the water and, after a little more than two and a quarter somersaults, snap out into the extended position for the entry, legs up and arms moving forward to line up the entry. Always *see* the water over the tops of the hands before the entry.

Points To Remember

1. *Always* lower the head and arms before the feet leave the board. If you wait too long, the tendency is to draw the legs, that is, for the legs to move up to the arms as the arms move down to grasp the legs.

2. Roll the entry if it is necessary. (See Chapter 21, Saving Dives.) A saved or rolled entry works very well on forward spinning dives.

7.1
Forward one-and-a-half tuck. See the water.

7.2
Forward double tuck. Arching the body adjusts for the proper entry.

Three-and-a-Half Somersault Tuck (Three-Meter)

The mechanics and the technique of this dive are exactly the same as the previous dive, the two-and-a-half. The difference is one of degree.

Directions to the Diver

During the takeoff you must push harder with the feet, both down and forward, and lower the upper body (head and arms) farther and faster. The tuck must be early and tight.

The entry procedure is identical with the two-and-a-half, with this exception. Usually, since the three-and-a-half must be started with a great deal of spin (a larger amount of angular momentum) and angular momentum is conserved, it is likely that the diver will have a great deal more spin left on the entry than in the two-and-a-half. This often makes the rolled entry essential. Sometimes it is impossible to get a clean entry without rolling. Don't be afraid to learn and use this very useful device.

Forward Spinning Dives in Pike Position

In many ways pike spinning dives are easier to control than tuck dives because the diver is better able to see where he is. The disadvantage of the pike position as compared to tuck is that for a given amount of spin the speed of the spin can never be as fast. Consequently, the number of somersaults easily done when the pike position is chosen is limited. However, at the current rate of progress it would not be surprising to see the three-and-a-half somersault done in pike position. Certainly many divers easily do the two-and-a-half pike from the one-meter board, a dive that was considered impossible not too many years ago.

Starting Pike Spins: The pike spinning dives *must* be started from the board with a more pronounced bend than in the tuck dives. This is particularly true of the multiple spinning dives.

Closed or Open Pike: The acceptable positions are the open pike and the closed pike, as previously described. For more than a one-and-a-half, the closed-pike position is used because the spin is faster.

7.3
Front somersault pike.

7.3

Front Somersault Pike

In general, divers should avoid doing feet-first-entry dives in competition. They are difficult to control and consequently seldom get good scores. However, a beginner who cannot do a one-and-a-half would do well to use a front somersault pike rather than tuck. It's easier.

Directions to the Diver

Land on the board straight. As it lifts, push forward with the feet and start into the pike, easily, before the feet leave the board. After completing about three quarters of a somersault, look for the water. (7.3)

For the entry, drop the legs and place the arms to the sides. Play the entry a bit short and then correct, if needed, by arching the body slightly during the entry.

Points To Remember

1. Take the dive up. Don't start the upper body down too soon or too hard for one somersault.

2. Play the entry short with a slightly arched body position. Increase the arch if needed.

Forward One-and-a-Half Somersault Pike

Divers have the option of doing the one-and-a-half somersault in either an open- or closed-pike position.

Directions to the Diver

Keep the head down throughout the takeoff and move easily into a tight pike position on the way up. Place the arms immediately in their position as the feet leave the board—either out to the sides at right angles to the body in open-pike position (7.4, next page) or grasping the legs just behind the knees in the closed-pike position. (7.5)

At the completion of little more than one somersault, look for the water. After you see it, easily open the pike for the entry by moving the legs up and back and the arms *forward* and down to line up for the entry.

Controlling the Amount of Spin Started: If a diver gets sufficient lift, not too much forward spin need be started from the board. It is to the diver's advantage to start without a great deal of angular momentum. He will be able to get a more vertical entry since there will be little spin left. (This is due to the conservation of angular momentum. If the diver leaves the board with the arms overhead and the body fairly straight, when he stretches for the entry his body position will be approximately the same as it was at the start, and he will be spinning approximately as fast.)

Points To Remember

1. Although some lean is necessary, start with the minimum amount.

2. Move the head and arms down and push *forward, before* the feet leave the board.

3. Always look for, and *see,* the water before the entry.

7.5
Forward one-and-a-half closed pike, one-meter board. (Diver is Frank Manheim.)

7.5

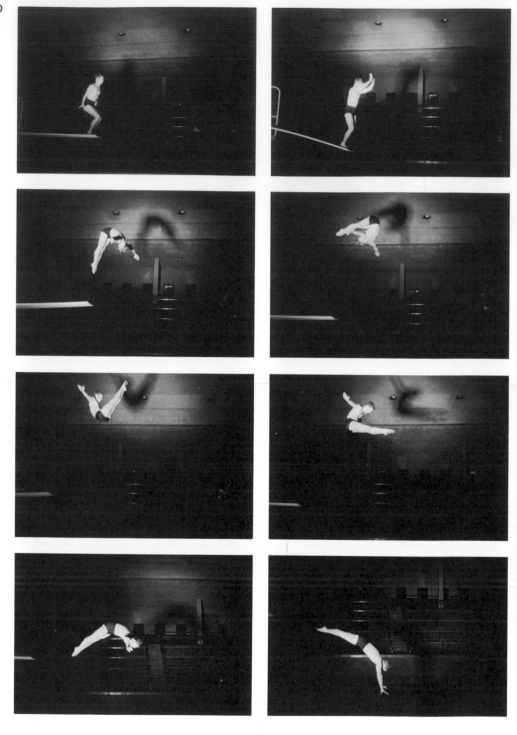

7.4
Forward one-and-a-half, three-meter board. (Diver
is Holt Maness.)

Forward Two-and-a-Half Somersault Pike

The method of doing this dive is much the same as the two-and-a-half somersault tuck. The obvious difference affecting the speed of the spin is the position. Since we know that angular momentum must be established before the feet leave the board, the focus is clearly on what the diver does before he is in the air.

Directions to the Diver

After the board is pressed, push down and *forward* with the feet (toward the water) and move the upper body down *as the board lifts*. Don't wait. (7.6)

Lift the hips and move *quickly* into a tight closed-pike position. Squeeze the pike tightly by pulling the head close to the legs, but keep looking for the water over the feet. When you see the water after two somersaults, open the pike and move the arms *forward* to line up the entry, which is short of vertical, to allow for the remaining spin. Use the somersault (roll) save if needed.

Using the One-Meter Board: More forward

spin is needed. Start with more lean than from the three-meter board and start the head, arms, and upper body down *immediately*. Lift only the hips—*never* try to get lift by lifting the head and arms during the takeoff.

Points To Remember

1. Always push *forward* (toward the tip of the board) during the takeoff.

2. Start the upper body down vigorously and *early*.

3. Squeeze the pike tightly for maximum spin velocity.

4. From the one-meter board use the roll entry if needed.

7.6

Forward two-and-a-half pike. Start to move the upper body down *as* the board lifts.

From the same back stance, whether a diver spins backward or inward depends on the direction in which his upper body is moving and the direction in which he pushes with his feet as he leaves the board. As in the forward spinning group of dives, the amount of backward spin a diver will get is determined *before* he is in the air.

Starting Backward Spin

A diver does three things to start backward spin:

1. He pushes back against the board with his feet.
2. He leans back slightly.
3. He circles his arms up and arches back during the takeoff.

The Push of the Feet: In *all* backward spinning dives (started without excessive lean), a diver pushes down and *back* toward the tip of the board as the board lifts him. (8.1b)

Although this is hard to visualize, keep in mind Newton's third law. If the feet push down and back against the board, the opposite reaction will lift the legs and move them forward—starting backward spin.

(Although the diver is not aware of it, this push back is used on *all* back spinning dives.)

Lean: Moving the center of gravity back before taking off—leaning—is essential to avoid hitting the board and to help start the back spin. It is easy to see how leaning back could start the body spinning, just as the pencil balanced on a finger would spin if lifted sharply after it starts to fall. However, relying on a "falling-back" lean for spin would result in a dive that moves far out and has little lift.

To keep a dive a close but safe distance from the board, a diver should get his lean by sitting back, moving the hips back rather than the shoulders. An additional advantage of the "sitting-back" method is that the diver is in the normal jumping position. (8.1a) Try jumping up from the ground without flexing the hips (sitting the hips back). You will see how difficult it is to jump up effectively.

Earlier we talked about how the feet press back on back takeoffs. In addition to starting backward spin, this push also moves the body in the opposite direction (closer to the board). This is another reason why it is imperative to lean for all back dives—more lean than would be needed for inward dives (where the feet push forward, moving the body *away* from the board).

8.1
The back takeoff: (a) Circle the arms up as the board is pressed and sit the hips back for the proper takeoff position. (b) The feet press *back* on the takeoff to help start backward spin.

8.1   a   b

When the upper body lifts and arches back, angular momentum is introduced backward and is transferred to the whole body as it goes into the air. Although this arching is necessary for layout spins, take sparing advantage of the technique for tuck or pike dives. A pronounced arch back causes a "whip spin," that is, excessive spin and a diminished lift.

As the diver presses the board, the arms should circle down and around behind the body and up in front over the head. When the circling arms stop, their angular momentum is transferred to the body. Thus, if the diver intends doing many backward somersaults, as in a back two-and-a-half somersault, the arms must be circled very rapidly; whereas in a single back somersault the arms would circle more slowly and in a back dive, more slowly still. Difficulty in getting enough spin for a backward dive can often be corrected merely by speeding up the circling of the arms.

Changing the Velocity of the Spin

As in the forward spinning dives, angular momentum backward is determined and conserved once the feet have left the board. However, by bringing the body mass closer to the axis of rotation, you can speed up the spin. By lengthening the body, you slow down the spin. This means that for a given angular momentum a diver will spin fastest in a tuck, more slowly in a pike, and slowest in the layout position. It also means that for a back one-and-a-half somersault layout considerably more angular momentum would be needed than for the same dive in a tuck.

Conservation of Angular Momentum; Its Effect on the Entry

Since angular momentum is conserved, a diver *always* has some spin left, even when the body is straightened. This must be taken into account, and all back spinning dives should enter the water short of vertical to allow for this remaining spin. In addition, the body should *always* continue to turn underwater only in the direction of the spin in order to have a clean, splashless entry.

Back Dive Layout

The simplicity and grace of the back dive layout gives it the same appeal as the swan dive. (9.1)

Directions to the Diver

After the standard back press of the board, reach up and lift the chest, keeping the head in line. Squeeze the buttocks tightly, extend the legs, and point the toes.

In the air, immediately assume an inverted swan position (chest arched, arms out to the sides, abdomen flat) and hold it until you see the water. When the body is slightly short of vertical, stretch for the entry and eliminate most of the arch. Continue to turn underwater in the direction of the spin.

Mechanics of the Dive

Helping the Spin: During the takeoff the arms circle backward and up, and when they stop, the body starts to spin (transfer of angular momentum). Consequently, circling the arms faster can correct the problem of insufficient spin.

Controlling the Dive in the Air: Since the rules demand that the swan position be maintained in the air, a diver has little opportunity to correct errors once his feet have left the board. There are only two acceptable ways to speed up or slow the spin: increase the arch in the back to speed up spin (and vice versa); move the arms close to, or farther from, the axis of rotation.

For example, if the diver feels he has too much spin, he can gradually eliminate the arch and extend the arms from the swan position to overhead to slow the spin down acceptably.

Entry

There should be a slight arch (in the chest) so that the body position will match the curved entry line.

The diver should *always* continue to turn underwater so that he will hit the bottom of the pool closer to the board than when he entered. Although this is the principle of saving dives, used in moderation it is good practice for *all* backward spinning entries.

Points To Remember

1. Lay the head gently back when leaving the board. A fast head action will result in too much spin.

2. Place the arms in position *immediately*. Look back easily and keep the body firm.

3. Use the position of the arms and the amount of arch to control the spin. (See Chapter 21, Saving Dives.)

4. *See the water.*

5. Always continue turning underwater.

9.1
Back dive layout.

36 Back Dive Pike

A diver has the choice of doing the back dive using either a layout or pike position. The positions are quite different in feeling—the layout is more graceful, while the pike has precision and a gymnastic quality. (9.2)

Directions to the Diver

Sit the hips back and reach up as you depress the diving board. *Keep the head in line* and the body straight as the board lifts. Reach.

Pike early and tightly *on the way up;* hold the pike position momentarily. Open the pike easily, looking back to see the water. Then reach back with the arms to line up for the stretch and entry. Continue to turn underwater. (9.3)

9.2
The correct pike position

Mechanics of the Dive

Initial Spin: The speed of the spin increases when the pike position is taken. Therefore considerably less angular momentum (initial spin) is needed than for the same dive in the layout position.

Starting with a small amount of initial spin makes a more vertical entry possible since the same small amount of spin will be left.

Doing the Dive on the Way Up: Since the spin, lift, and distance cannot be altered in the air, the pike should start early to give the dive a long drop. This is an attractive style and one that gives more time to adjust for a good entry.

Playing the Dive Over: When the pike position is opened, the legs will move back away from the body (Newton's third law). Most divers open the dive when the legs are short of vertical. This makes the dive even shorter, and in order to get even a moderately good entry, the diver must arch. Whereas if the dive is played slightly over, the legs will move back to the vertical position, and an arched entry will not be necessary.

"Stopping" the Spin: Stopping the spin for the entry is accomplished by opening the pike and extending the arms overhead. When the body is straight, the spin will be slowest. A diver can use the length of time he holds the pike to control the entry, just as he did in the jackknife.

If he is spinning too fast, he straightens sooner, and if he has too little spin, he holds the pike a longer time. The legs can be *held* vertically if *after* the body is straightened the arms are circled back and overhead to line up with the body for the entry.

Remember from the Directions to the Diver that the sequence for lining up the entry was to open the pike, *then* reach back. The reason for circling the arms back after the body is straight is to keep the straightened body from going over and the legs stationary. Even after the pike is opened, the body will continue to spin, although much more slowly. By circling the arms back overhead, a counterforce is introduced to the spinning body, and the legs stay in the same place.

Points To Remember

1. Keep the backward lean to a minimum. However, more lean is needed for this dive than for an inward dive. Use the hip lean.

2. Reach up, but keep the head in line with the body. If the head is whipped back, excessive spin results, and the lift is cut.

3. Play the dive slightly long. After the touch hold the pike momentarily.

4. The entry angle should be almost vertical—always continue turning underwater.

9.3
Back dive pike.

10.1
Back one-and-a-half tuck. Diver is National Champion, Chuck Knorr.

Back One-and-a-Half Somersault Tuck

Directions to the Diver

Tuck early and tightly on the way up. Keep the head in line with the body and don't look back excessively during the takeoff or the spin.

After one somersault, kick the legs up and out into a pike position. Drop away from the legs, with the head back to see the water; then place the arms back to line up the entry. The body should be in a slightly chest-arched position. (10.1)

Learning To Know When To Open the Tuck:

After one somersault, back spinning dives tend to be blind because it is difficult for the diver to fix his eyes on an object (the board, the wall, the ceiling, and so forth) while he is spinning. He often learns to feel rather than to see when to come out of the tuck. Through practice he learns to use the speed of the spin, the time gone by, and the amount of lift as gauges. However, it is possible and *advisable* to try to spot the back end of the board or the wall after one somersault. A diver can train himself to do this and, whenever possible, should *see* where he is.

Stopping the Backward Spin: The method used to stop this dive successfully is the same as that used in the back dive pike. (10.2) After one somersault the diver spots the wall and kicks the legs out of the tuck into a pike. He can then keep the legs stationary by straightening the body as he looks for the water and by bringing the arms back to line up the entry.

Remember—a spin can never be completely stopped, only slowed down.

Legs First: When a diver has completed slightly more than one somersault, his thighs are in the correct entry position. (10.2e) By straightening the lower legs into a pike, he puts his legs at the proper angle for an entry. (10.2f)

Looking Back: When a diver straightens out of a pike position and looks back for the water, his legs and upper body move in opposite directions, and movement of the legs in the direction of the spin is canceled out; they remain stationary. (10.2f, g)

Now, because the body is straight, the spin will be slower. In order to keep the legs and the straightened body from spinning and to prevent the dive from going over, the arms circle back toward the water. In the same way as opening the pike prevented the legs from turning, the circling of the arms prevents the body from turning. (10.2g, h) The fact that the legs stay in one place for so long gives the illusion that the dive is finished long before it actually is and makes for a more appealing dive.

Margin for Error

The described method of coming out of a back one-and-a-half somersault tuck makes it possible to correct errors of judgment. For example, if the diver realizes he will be "short" (not have enough spin), he can keep his arms down at his sides as he looks back and *arches* his body to speed up the spin. If he realizes he will have too much spin, he makes himself as long as possible by straightening the body and circling the arms back very quickly to slow his spin down early in the dive.

Points To Remember

1. Never throw the head back or arch excessively at the start of the dive. It gives whip spin which is difficult to stop and cuts the lift.

2. Always kick the legs out of the tuck first; then look back and circle the arms to stop the spin.

3. Always continue to turn underwater.

10.2
Back one-and-a-half tuck showing the kickout into
pike position.

Back Two-and-a-Half Somersault Tuck

The technique used for a back two-and-a-half somersault tuck is identical with the back one-and-a-half. The only difference is that more initial spin (angular momentum) is needed to make it around for the additional somersault.

Increasing the Angular Momentum

The spin is started as in the back one-and-a-half but with greater force because more spin is needed. Since the diver must get good lift and stay reasonably close to the board, the amount of lean is not changed. Rather, the spin is increased by circling the arms very rapidly and pushing back very hard with the feet during the takeoff.

Spinning Early

It is pointless to tuck late because the amount of spin was determined when the feet left the board. Therefore, the wise diver moves into the tuck position immediately on the way up. The earlier he tucks, the sooner in the dive he will complete the required number of somersaults.

Using a Saved Entry

Since the dive starts with a large amount of spin or angular momentum, there will be considerable spin left during the entry, even when the body is fully stretched. Angular momentum is conserved; it can never be stopped. The diver, therefore, *must* continue to turn underwater in the direction of the spin to make a good entry: the entry must be saved. (See Chapter 21, Saving Dives.)

Points To Remember

1. Always sit the hips back as the board is pressed to get the *necessary* lean and to put yourself in the correct jumping position.

2. Do not whip the head back or arch too much to start the spin. Rather, circle the arms rapidly and push back hard against the board with the feet.

3. Always squeeze the tuck tightly.

4. Always save the entry.

Back Somersault Pike

This is a very simple dive. (10.3) Follow these steps: reach; pike on the way up; see the water; stretch for the entry.

Control the spin by the speed with which you circle the arms up on the takeoff (faster if more spin is needed). Control the entry by the length of time the pike position is held. Remember to keep the head in line at the start of the dive and to enter the water slightly short of vertical with the body at an attention position.

10.3

Back somersault pike. Reach up, pike early and tightly on the way up, and *see* the water to judge the entry.

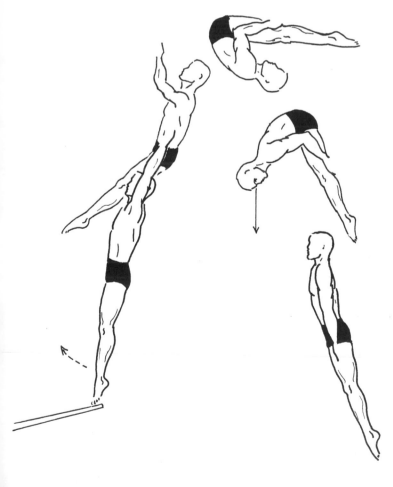

Directions to the Diver
Circle the arms up rapidly as the board is pressed and when it rises, lift the chest and head. *Do not throw the head back.* (10.4a, b) As soon as the feet leave the board, quickly lift the legs up into a tight pike. After one somersault, *see the board* (10.4e); place the legs in entry position using the board as a gauge. Look back for the water and circle the arms back to line up for the entry (10.4f, g), which will be short of vertical. Always save the dive, using the scooped entry as needed, depending on the amount of spin left.

Avoiding a Head-Back Position: A dive done in a pike position requires more spin backward from the board than a tuck. At the start of the dive, however, the head should not be thrown back excessively. Although this movement will increase the spin, the result is a "whipping" spin (too much initial spin with little lift) and difficulty in spotting the board after the first somersault.

Transfer of Angular Momentum from the Arms: Instead of using a deep arch and head-back position to get spin, the diver should concentrate on the circling of the arms. The faster the arms are circled, the greater the initial spin momentum of the dive.

Conserving the Spin: The diver will have about as much spin during the entry as he did when he left the board because at both times the body position is almost the same—fully extended, arms overhead. Clearly, in order to enter the water without excessive spin, one should start with the least amount of spin necessary to a successful dive. This can only be achieved by practice.

Spinning on the Way Up: If the dive starts with the minimum required spin and the pike position is taken immediately after the feet leave the board, the result is a "finished" dive, spun on the way up with a long drop to the water.

Spotting for the Entry: At the completion of one somersault, the diver *sees* the board or the wall behind the board. He uses this as a gauge to determine where he is in the dive, how far he has spun, and how high he has completed the first somersault. This helps him to decide when to open the pike and reach the arms back to slow down the spin for the entry.

Points To Remember
1. Always get into the pike early, on the way up, in order to finish the dive and have a drop to the water for the entry.

2. Always spot the board after one somersault.

3. Always use a saved or scooped entry underwater.

10.4
Back one-and-a-half pike.

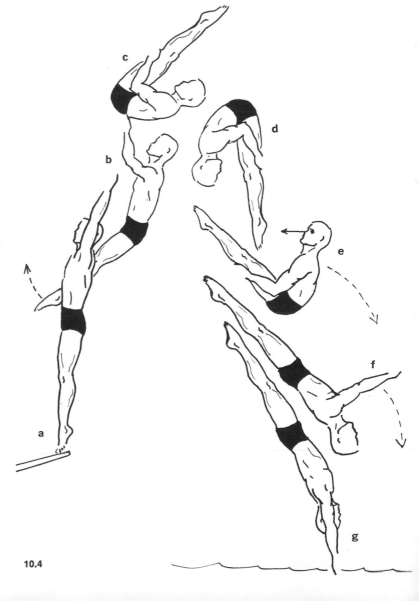

10.4

10.6
Proper start of a back somersault layout. Notice that the diver sees the water just after his feet leave the board. (Diver is Fletcher Gilders, former N.C.A.A. and A.A.U. Champion.)

Back Somersault Layout

Directions to the Diver
Lean back as the board is pressed. As it lifts, arch and reach back, extend the legs, and move the head sharply back. (10.5) (Do all this before the feet leave the board.) Take a swan position with the head back, seeing the water almost immediately. (10.6) During the drop for the entry, eliminate most of the arch and slowly bring the arms down to the sides. Enter short of vertical with the head up.

Controlling the Spin; Correcting Errors
While maintaining the layout position, errors in judgment of spin can be corrected only by increasing or decreasing the amount of body arch (to speed up or slow down the spin) and by bringing the arms closer to, or farther from, the axis of rotation. Only these two things will acceptably change the speed of the spin after the diver is in the air, and their use is limited.

Looking for the Water
The diver should see the water early before half of a somersault is completed to control the dive for a proper entry.

Points To Remember
1. Always arch and look back to see the water as you take off from the board. Use a high chest arch; it will give you maximum lift as well as spin.

2. Always play the entry slightly short. When this dive is over, you've had it.

3. Increase the arch if there is not enough spin (never pike) and straighten out if there is too much spin.

4. Always place the arms to the sides during the entry. Do this later if the dive is spinning too fast and earlier if there is not enough spin.

10.5
Back somersault layout.

10.7

Back One-and-a-Half Somersault Layout

Although usually done from the three-meter board, this dive can be competently done from the low board. (10.7) A successfully executed back one-and-a-half layout from the one-meter board *demands* the use of a saved entry due to the large amount of spin that has to be initiated from the board. A degree of saving is needed even from the three-meter board.

Directions to the Diver

Lean back and circle the arms rapidly *up* as the board is pressed. Start a fast first somersault by reaching back, lifting the chest, and snapping the head back. Press firmly back against the board (toward the tip) as it lifts. (All this must be done before the feet leave the board.) (10.8) In the air bring the arms immediately down to the waist. (Note that the arms have begun to move down even before the feet have left the board.) Assume the proper layout position. (10.9)

See the board, "checking" the dive as needed. Look back for the water while circling the arms back to line up for the entry. Always keep turning underwater *only* in the direction of the spin.

Spinning on the Way Up

In a back one-and-a-half somersault layout, the problem for the diver is to get sufficient spin without sacrificing lift. It is very easy to spin fast if an excessive lean is taken. However, this cuts the lift considerably. Ideally, the dive should go high and spin quickly on the way up.

To achieve the preferred style, the diver keeps the lean to a minimum and depends on the fast circling of the arms, the fast movement of the head back, plus a firm press back against the board to supply the spin. With this starting technique the flight of the dive is high, close to the board, and the first somersault is fast and early.

As soon as the feet leave the board, the arms are quickly brought down to the waist. This immediately speeds up the spin because the moment of inertia is decreased.

10.7
Back one-and-a-half layout: (a) After half a somersault the diver *sees* the board. (b) Look back to see the water. (c) Proper angle of entry.
10.8
The takeoff for a back one-and-a-half layout.
10.9
Back one-and-a-half layout. The correct body position.

10.8, 10.9

Checking the Dive—Seeing the Board

The diver can slow down the spin by eliminating the body arch (a high chest arch). He can learn to see the board after less than half a somersault is completed. (10.7) Then he checks the dive by eliminating some of the arch and the head-back position, while watching the board.

The diver uses the level of the board to help determine what point he has reached in the dive. For example, if he sees the board well below him, he knows he has completed the first somersault early and that he has enough time to look back slowly for the entry. On the other hand, if the level of the board is higher, he knows that he has less time and space to complete the rest of the dive. He must immediately look back and increase the body arch to speed up the spin in order to make it around.

Using the Arms To Slow Down and Control the Spin: The diver first sees the board and then looks back to see the water, keeping the arms pressed against his waist. When the correct entry position is anticipated, he circles his arms back to line up for the entry. (10.7)

Because the arms are circled back, the body will react by moving in the opposite direction, which cancels out some of its spin. When the arms stop, the spin begins again, although more slowly (since the arms are in an extended position overhead).

If the diver realizes that he is spinning too fast when he spots the board, he should circle the arms back and overhead early to slow the spin down. If he feels he is spinning too slowly, he keeps the arms at the waist for as long as possible and increases his body arch to get the maximum spin for the longest time.

The Entry

The angle of the body *must* be short of vertical during the entry, and the body *must* turn underwater in the direction of the spin. (10.7)

Points To Remember

1. *Always* take a slight backward lean.

2. Try to get a fast first somersault on the way up by arching and looking back on the take-off. Make sure the arch is a high chest arch (not a belly arch) for maximum lift.

3. Bring the arms down to the waist early and quickly—as soon as you leave the board—to speed up the spin.

4. *Always* check the board. Look for it and see it after the first somersault. Use it as a gauge.

5. Try to see the water as you circle the arms back for the entry.

6. *Always save the entry.*

Starting Reverse Spin

After a forward approach, whether a diver spins forward or reverse depends primarily on the direction in which his feet push against the lifting board.

As previously explained, to spin forward the feet *must* push forward—toward the tip of the board. To spin reverse, the opposite is true: the feet must push *backward* against the lifting board during the takeoff (toward the back end of the board—away from the water). (11.1) As a result of this push back (according to Newton's third law), the legs are moved forward, turning the body in a reverse direction. Also the entire body is moved in the direction opposite to the push, that is, away from the board.

The Takeoff Angle for Reverse Dives

Because of the difference in the direction of the push for forward and reverse spinning dives, it follows that there must be a corresponding difference in the angle of takeoff for both dives. Since in reverse dives the push back moves the body away from the board, considerably less forward lean is needed than for a forward spinning dive, in which a push *forward* tends to move the body back toward the diving board. The angle of takeoff used for forward spinning dives would be incorrect for reverse dives; there would be too much lean.

11.1
Takeoff for reverse spinning dives. The diver's feet push *back* against the board (heavy arrow), and the reaction lifts the legs and starts the reverse spin.

11.2

A "Checked Hurdle"

A checked hurdle is one in which the diver depends on the forward momentum of the hurdle plus the push back against the board to carry him out. Consequently he lands on the end of the board feeling as though he is leaning almost backward. (11.2)

The proper takeoff for a reverse spinning dive has the following elements: a push backward against the board combined with a lifting of the head, chest, and arms; a complete extension of the legs and toes with a tight squeezing of the buttocks. Although the head is lifted on the takeoff, it is never thrown back except for layout spinning dives when the head *is* snapped back immediately to start the spin. (11.3)

Transfer of Angular Momentum

One technique that controls and initiates reverse spin is the circling of the arms as the board is pressed. On all takeoffs, the arms *circle* back down and around behind the body and up in front. When they stop, their angular momentum is transferred to the body. The faster the arms are circled, the greater the momentum. Therefore, in reverse dives requiring great amounts of spin (as in a two-and-a-half), the arms should circle very quickly; in a reverse somersault tuck, more slowly; and in a reverse dive pike, slower still.

Controlling the Speed of the Spin

The angular momentum (the amount of spin) is determined and conserved once the feet leave the board. However, the *speed* of the spin can be changed in the air.

Increasing and Decreasing the Moment of Inertia: Keep in mind that the same principle that changes the speed of forward spinning dives applies to *all* spinning dives. Briefly, controlling the speed of the spin depends on the distance of the mass from the spinning axis (the radius of gyration). Compare a reverse dive layout and a reverse somersault tuck. In the somersault the spin will speed up considerably when the tuck is taken (the radius of gyration is shortened). Whereas in the layout dive where this cannot be done, divers will need more spin to begin with (more angular momentum). Similarly, in a reverse one-and-a-half somersault tuck, the spin speeds up when the diver tucks and slows down when he comes out of the tuck for the entry (lengthens the radius).

Entries

For all reverse dives the angle of entry is slightly short of vertical to allow for the spin that is always left. Also, every reverse dive should continue to turn underwater *only* in the direction of the spin.

11.2
The checked hurdle, as demonstrated by Ken Sitzberger.
11.3
The takeoff into a reverse spinning dive in the layout position.

11.3

Reverse Dive Layout

Many people consider this the most beautiful dive of all. It is extremely graceful, dramatic, easy for spectators to follow, and for the diver, a very satisfying dive if done well. (12.1)

Directions to the Diver

Check the hurdle. Immediately after leaving the board, lift the chest and place the raised arms out to the sides at right angles to the body and in line with the shoulders. Lay the head back, and "chest arch" slightly. *Look for the water* and stretch for the entry, eliminating most of the arch. (12.2) Always turn underwater in the direction of the spin.

Mechanics of the Dive

If you were to jump forward from the ground making the legs move forward faster than the upper body, you would be doing what a diver does when he starts a reverse dive layout. Try this several times and analyze what you do. There is no doubt that you push *back* very hard against the ground and that you must have only a *slight* forward lean, exactly as during the final lift of the board in reverse spinning dives.

Increasing or Decreasing the Speed of the Spin: If a diver is having difficulty spinning fast enough, he can often correct this deficiency by speeding up the circling of the arms as the board is pressed.

In the air there are two things he can do to vary the spin: change the position of the arms, and vary the amount of body arch. If he has too little spin, his arms should remain out to the sides (close to the spinning axis), and the arch of the body should be increased immediately. Arching the back speeds up the spin, which should be a high chest arch.

If there is too much spin, the arch should be eliminated and the arms moved together over the head early in the dive, lengthening the body.

The Entry

When the body is straightened and stretched for the entry, the spin stops. However, since there will always be some spin left, the body should *continue to turn underwater.*

Points To Remember

1. *Check* the hurdle; very little forward lean.

2. Start the dive from the board: press back with the feet; lift the chest; squeeze the buttocks. (12.1)

3. Look back to see the water.

4. Play the dive slightly long—you can always stretch to stop the spin.

5. Enter looking at the entry point. Always continue to turn a little underwater.

12.1
Reverse dive layout. The checked hurdle with the feet pushing *back* on takeoff.

12.2
The correct position for a reverse dive layout. (Photo by D. A. Cahlander)

12.1

12.2

12.3

Reverse Dive Pike

The required reverse dive may be done either layout or pike, at the option of the diver. The pike position has an exciting quality the layout dive lacks.

Directions to the Diver

Check the hurdle. In the air bring the legs up to the hands quickly and keep the head in line with the body. Look at the toes as you touch and touch before the peak of the lift. Squeeze the pike, then "leave" the legs by dropping the body back and away; *look* for the water. Stretch for the entry (12.3) and turn underwater in the direction of the spin.

Need for Less Angular Momentum

The major difference between the start of the reverse dive layout and the reverse dive pike is that considerably *less* reverse spin is needed for the pike dive. Therefore, on the takeoff the head and chest are not moved back: the body is in a straight line as it goes into the air, with little if any arch.

Completing the Pike on the Way Up

Many divers reach up and wait before piking, thinking they will go higher. This is not true because the amount of lift has been predetermined by the time the feet have left the board. Therefore it is logical to bring the legs up early so that the dive may be completed at the peak of the lift. This allows a long drop to the water and a finished, better-looking dive.

Playing the Dive Over

After the touch, when the body drops away from the legs for the entry, the legs will move back in the opposite direction. To allow for this, the pike position should be held until the legs are vertical, thereby preventing a short dive. (12.4)

Controlling the Spin

The length of time that the pike is held can be used to control the dive. If a diver feels he has developed too much spin, he should touch and open the pike quickly and early. If he feels that his spin is slow, the correction is to hold the pike as long as needed, until the legs are in entry position.

The Entry

The angle of entry should be very close to vertical to take into account the movement of the dive away from the board and the small amount of remaining spin. The dive continues underwater.

Points To Remember

1. Check the hurdle.

2. Reach up. Keep the head in line. Do not look back on the way up.

3. Touch the toes on the way up. Don't wait too long.

12.3
Reverse dive pike. Perfect execution by Lou Vitucci.
12.4
The vertical touch for the reverse dive pike, one-meter board.

12.4

Reverse Somersault Tuck

Although most competitors avoid the use of feet-first-entry dives, novices often do the reverse somersault because it is an easy dive to learn.

Directions to the Diver

As you leave the board, feel as though you are reaching up for a bar about three feet in front and ten feet above the end of the board. (13.1) On the way up, tuck tightly but *do not throw the head back*. Look for the water to gauge the entry and open the tuck by moving the legs down and slightly back. Straighten the body with the arms to the sides and enter almost vertically, head up, and body slightly arched.

Speed of Spin at the Entry: The speed of the spin will be *greater* during the entry than it was at the start of this dive if the diver left the board in the proper position with his arms above his head. When the arms are lowered to the sides for the entry (to comply with the rules), the radius of gyration decreases, and to conserve angular momentum, the spin velocity increases. (Angular momentum equals moment of inertia times angular velocity. Remember, moment of inertia is m times r^2. Since the diver established the angular momentum of the dive as he left the board with his body extended, arms up, when he lowers his arms for the entry, the moment of inertia decreases and, therefore, the spin velocity increases. If he entered arms overhead, the spin velocity would be the same. That's why you see a diver involuntarily lift his arms to stop a reverse somersault from going over.) There is little the diver can do to control or limit the speed of the spin during the entry. Therefore, he must *start* the dive with the *least possible* angular momentum. Then, when the arms are at the sides and the body straightened for the entry, he will not be turning excessively.

Nevertheless there will be some rotation left. Starting the entry slightly short of vertical allows for this remaining spin.

Points To Remember

1. *Never* throw the head back at the start of the dive; it results in too much spin and cuts the lift.

2. Look for the water. Make sure to see it after three quarters of a somersault to gauge the entry properly.

13.1
Reverse somersault tuck.

13.2   a   b   c   d   e

13.3

Reverse One-and-a-Half Somersault Tuck

Directions to the Diver

Circle the arms up quickly as the board is depressed. When the board lifts, reach up, lift the chest, and keep the head in line. Don't look back. (13.2b)

Without waiting, tuck tightly (13.2c) and after one somersault kick the legs sharply up and out of the tuck into a pike position. (13.2d) Then look back to see the water, straightening the body. Finally reach back with the arms to line up for the entry. (13.2e)

Always continue to turn underwater.

Mechanics of the Dive

A forward-moving hurdle provides enough forward momentum to move the diver away from the board. He feels safe and can concentrate all his efforts on getting lift. (Note the length of Clotworthy's hurdle in 13.2.)

Although the tuck position should be taken on the way up, the diver must be careful not to leave the board with his knees bending. This would eliminate some of the push down and cut the lift of the dive considerably. The idea is to reach up while pushing down hard and *then* get into the tuck position immediately. (13.3)

Stopping the Spin: After the tuck is taken, the dive is executed in a manner similar to the back one-and-a-half somersault tuck. A little after one somersault, the legs are kicked out and up into a pike position (13.2d); then the diver straightens his body and looks back. Finally, he extends the arms back for the entry. (Note in 13.2 that the legs have remained in about the same position from the kickout until the entry into the water.)

The final stretch for the entry results in the slowest possible spin.

Points To Remember

1. *Always* get into the tuck position quickly without snapping the head back.

2. *Always* kick the legs out of the tuck first; then look back and straighten the body; and finally, stretch for the entry.

3. Always turn underwater in the direction of the spin. *Always*.

13.2
Reverse one-and-a-half tuck by Olympic Champion Bob Clotworthy. A good illustration of the checked hurdle takeoff and the pike kickout.
13.3
From a checked hurdle, reverse spin starts immediately.

Reverse Two-and-a-Half Somersault Tuck

Mechanics of the Dive

The mechanics of this dive are almost identical with the reverse one-and-a-half tuck. However, since it requires more spin (angular momentum), there is a slight difference in technique as the board is lifting (before the diver is in the air). (13.4)

Leaving the Board: There must be a very rapid circling of the arms on the takeoff, and the feet must push back with great intensity against the lifting board.

Tucking Early and Tightly: The tuck position should be taken very early (as soon as the feet leave the board) and should be as tight as possible for maximum speed of spin.

Saving the Entry: Due to the conservation of angular momentum, there is a lot of spin left during the entry because a large initial spinning force was started from the board. This can *never* be eliminated and *demands* the use of the saved or scooped entry. (See Chapter 21 on Saving Dives.) The diver necessarily continues to turn underwater *only* in the direction of the spin.

13.4
Reverse two-and-a-half tuck by Lou Vitucci.

13.4

Reverse Somersault Pike

Directions to the Diver
Reach! Pike early and tightly, but don't throw the head back. *See* the water (13.5) and open the pike for the entry, sliding the hands along the legs until the body is straight. Enter the water slightly short of vertical with the arms at the sides.

Points To Remember
1. Use a checked hurdle.

2. Circle the arms around and up faster than for a tuck dive to increase the amount of the spin.

3. Look for the water. Use it to control the opening of the pike for the entry.

Reverse One-and-a-Half Somersault Pike
Many divers and coaches feel that this dive (13.6, p. 56), when correctly done, is simpler to control than the reverse one-and-a-half tuck. The pike position makes it easier to see and to know when to open for the entry.

Directions to the Diver
Check the hurdle. (13.6a, b, c)

Circle the arms up quickly. As soon as the feet leave the board, pike, keeping the head in line; do not whip the head back. (13.6f) Squeeze the pike. After one somersault spot the other end of the pool. (13.6k)

Open the pike with the head back to see the water (13.6m), then circle the arms back to line up for the entry. (13.6n, o) *Always* turn underwater in the direction of the spin. (13.6p, q)

Seeing Where You Are: If the head is in line and not thrown back while spinning, it is quite simple to spot the opposite wall after completing the first somersault. When the diver learns to do this, he can gauge what point he has reached in the dive.

When his legs are in the proper entry position, he opens the pike, looks back to see the water, and then circles the arms back to line up for the entry. This accomplishes two things: it slows the spin (the radius of gyration increases); it keeps the legs stationary. Due to the action-reaction principle the circling of the arms presses the legs back in the opposite direction and temporarily stops the spin.

Points To Remember
1. Reach up; pike early. Keep the head in line.

2. Try to spot the other end of the pool after one somersault.

13.5
Reverse somersault pike.

Reverse Somersault Layout

All feet-first dives are difficult to do well (judges seldom give good scores for feet-first dives), particularly when the layout position is chosen. In the pike dive the pike can be held longer if there is not enough spin or opened sooner if there is too much spin. The rules demand that layout position must be held from start to finish. Therefore, the amount of spin must be very accurately started from the board, leaving little margin for error.

It is recommended that in competition this dive be used sparingly, if at all. (13.7)

Directions to the Diver

You *must* use a checked hurdle. Before the feet leave the board look back quickly, reach up and back, and arch the body.

Bring the arms down to the sides immediately and look for the water. Eliminate most of the arch during the drop and entry.

It is almost impossible to do this dive with the same takeoff angle used for a front dive. There would be entirely too much forward lean. Make sure to check the hurdle. (See "Checked Hurdle," Chapter 11.)

Controlling the Spin in the Air

As in all the layout spinning dives, once in the air the diver is limited to two acceptable methods of controlling his spin: changing the body arch and positioning the arms.

Playing the Dive Short

Since there is such a large angular momentum at the start of the dive, there will be lots of spin left during the entry. To allow for this, the angle of entry *must* be short of vertical.

Points To Remember

1. *Always* check the hurdle.

2. Always arch and look back *as the board is lifting*.

3. Bring the arms *down* to the sides early in the dive to speed up the spin.

4. Always look for the water and try to see it early.

13.7
Reverse somersault layout. Start the spin immediately.

13.7

a   b

e   f

i   j

m   n

13.6
Reverse one-and-a-half pike. Look for and *see* the other end of the pool.

q

57

c

d

g

h

k

l

o

p

Reverse One-and-a-Half Somersault Layout

The "gainer" one-and-a-half layout (13.8), as it used to be called, was traditionally considered the most difficult dive in the listed table. The modern aluminum boards have changed this, and the reverse one-and-a-half layout is used quite frequently in competition, and by girls as well as boys. Although it is performed exclusively from the three-meter board, it can be done from the one-meter.

Directions to the Diver

Check your hurdle. Circle the arms quickly and start the spin immediately; press *back* with the feet, whip the head back, and arch the upper back—all *before* the feet leave the board.

Bring the arms down to the waist *immediately* after leaving the board, increasing the arch. After one somersault, look back for the water; then stretch the arms back to line up for the entry.

Save the dive by turning underwater only in the direction of the spin. This *must* be done.

Controlling the Spin in the Air

Even before the feet leave the board, the arms should begin to move down toward the waist. In the air they must press close to the body to increase the speed of the spin.

The only other way a diver can speed up his spin is to increase the body arch, which is exactly what happens when a pike position is used to increase spin velocity. (The body mass moves closer to the axis of rotation.)

The Entry

As with the back one-and-a-half layout, it is essential to enter the water short of the vertical and to save the dive. It is impossible to take the dive straight down and get a good entry.

Points To Remember

1. Always circle the arms up very rapidly as the board is pressed.

2. Always start the spin vigorously from the board; *before* you are in the air, whip the head back, press back with the feet, and arch (make it a high chest arch, which looks better and is easier to control).

3. Always look back for the water and *then* bring the arms back for the entry. Circling the arms back helps to stop the spin.

4. *Always* save or scoop the entry.

13.8
Reverse one-and-a-half layout by Olympic diver Frank Gorman.

13.8

The force that starts a diver rotating inward must occur *while he is still on the board.*

Starting Inward Spin

There are certain problems that are unique for the inward spinning dives. How can a diver move away from the board backward and still safely spin inward? What starts the spin?

In forward spinning dives the lean forward helps to initiate the spin. For inward dives there obviously can be no forward lean. On the contrary there must be some movement back to avoid hitting the board.

Directing the Push of the Feet Against the Board: The direction in which the feet push against the lifting board determines whether the diver spins backward or inward. To spin inward, the feet *must push down and forward* (toward the back end of the board) as the board lifts. (14.1b) When the feet push in this way, then according to the third law the board pushes in the opposite direction, up and backward, which starts the body spinning inward. In an inward dive, layout position, since the head and chest are lifted, the push of the feet supplies *all* the torque, the force that causes turning around an axis.

Another Effect of the Push of the Feet: As well as starting inward spin, the push of the feet moves the body *away from the board.* Therefore, for inward dives less backward lean is needed than would be needed for back spinning dives.

Moving the Upper Body Down: For all inward dives, with the exception of the inward dive layout, the head and arms should be *moving down before* the feet leave the board. (14.2)

The movement of the upper body down while the feet are still in contact with the board introduces angular momentum (spin) in an inward direction, which is transferred to the whole body when it goes into the air. *to pg 62*

Getting Stuck: If the upper body is lowered *after* the diver is in the air, the legs will lift equally, resulting in "drawing the knees" or getting stuck (as explained in Chapter 5, Forward Spinning Dives: General Principles).

14.1

14.1
Proper takeoff for inward spinning dives: (a) Sit the hips back as the board is pressed but keep the head and shoulders over the board. (b) As the board lifts, push *forward* with the feet, lift the hips, and lower the head and arms.

14.2
The head, arms, and upper body *must be moving down before the feet leave the board* to start an inward one-and-a-half pike from the one-meter board.

14.2

Sitting Back; Using a Hip Lean: Since in the inward dives much of the movement away from the board is accomplished by the forward push of the feet, minimal backward lean is needed. But in order to get good lift and spin, the required *small* amount of lean should be taken by moving the hips back rather than the shoulders. If the diver leans by moving the shoulders back, a very common error, the dive moves out too far, and there is great difficulty in starting the spin. If, however, he uses the sitting-back method (14.3), not only does he move safely out but he is in the proper position for starting a good inward spin.

In 14.4, you can clearly see what happens when the legs are straightened from this sitting position. The forceful extension of the knees lifts the hips and causes the *necessary* push forward and down against the board. It is the reaction to this push that will move the diver safely away from the board as he starts a good inward spin. If the hips are kept forward as the board is pressed, the push will not be nearly as effective. Generally, in *all* inward spinning dives, (1) a sitting position, knees bent, hips back rather than shoulders, is assumed; (2) the feet push *forward* against the board to start the spin; (3) the head and arms move down as the board lifts.

Speeding Up and Slowing Down the Spin
As in the forward spinning dives, once the diver is in the air, the speed of the spin can be increased by bringing the body mass closer to the spinning axis. The tighter the tuck or pike, the faster the spin. (See Chapter 5, Forward Spinning Dives, General Principles.)

Entries
Every effort should be made to spin all inward dives on the way up and to finish the dive early, as a long drop to the water in the extended entry body position is desirable.

Inward dives should enter about vertically. This is to conform with the path of the center of gravity and to allow for the remaining spin. (See Chapter 20, Entries.) The somersault save is effective for inward dives.

14.3
Illustration of the sitting-back press to start inward spins.
14.4
The sitting-back press causes forward push as the legs straighten.

14.3

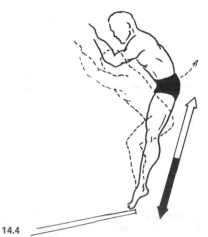

14.4

Inward Dive Pike

Despite the fact that the diver spins toward the board, the execution of the "back jackknife" poses the least number of problems for either the beginner or advanced diver. (15.1)

Directions to the Diver

Use the sitting back method of lean. Lift the hips and start the arms and head moving easily down as the board lifts. On the way up, *look at the water* and allow the hips to ride overhead as the touch is made. Hold a tight pike until the upper body has moved into the correct entry position. Then move the legs back and up and the *arms forward* to align the body for the vertical entry.

Moving the Weight Back; Leaning

One of the principal problems for this dive is to combine successfully inward spin, good lift, and movement back from the board. The diver should enter the water a comfortable distance from the board, about two feet. This is accomplished by the sit-back lean.

Getting Maximum Lift

If on the takeoff the upper body is lowered from the waist with the back straight, a good inward spin will result, but the lift will be poor. Whereas if the back is lifted in a round-shouldered manner, as the *head* moves down, considerably more lift will result and less spin. Since so little spin is required for this dive (after all, this is only half a somersault), it is advantageous to get the additional lift.

Points To Remember

1. Always use some hip lean; never lean the head and shoulders back. Don't "fall" off the board.

2. Always start the head and arms moving down before the feet leave the board. If you wait until you are in the air, a "stuck" spin results.

3. Look at the water through the entire dive. It gives you a reference to judge the entry.

4. Enter vertically.

15.1
Inward dive pike.

Inward Dive Layout

Directions to the Diver

The inward dive layout (15.2) is *impossible* to do well if a shoulder rather than a hip (sit-back) lean is used. Therefore make certain that the head and shoulders stay directly over the end of the board during the press. On the takeoff (as the board lifts), lift the head and chest and start the arms moving down to swan position. Push *forward very hard* against the surface of the board, keeping the head in line with the body. After leaving the board, arch the upper back slightly (chest arch), lift the legs up and back, and look straight ahead. Hold this position until the stretch for the vertical entry; then, looking at the water, move the arms together and eliminate the chest arch.

Starting the Spin

The inward dive layout is unique in that the diver gets no help from the lean, cannot bring the upper body down to help start the spin, and cannot whip the arms down. On the contrary, the upper body lifts, and the lean is taken in the wrong direction to start inward spin.

The Push of the Feet: The only way to start a good inward spin, while lifting the head and chest, is to push the feet *vigorously forward* toward the back end of the diving board as it lifts. Then, according to the third law the board will push back in the opposite direction. This moves the legs back and up, starts the spin inward, and also moves the body away from the board. Hence the diver can use *minimum* backward lean, less than would be required for a back spinning dive.

15.2
Inward dive layout.

Position in the Air

In the air the position must be held, and there can be no piking at the hips to increase the speed of the spin. (15.3) Clearly the initial spin, the angular momentum inward, must be well established from the board. Once in the air the diver can speed up his spin in only one acceptable way—increasing the body arch. Remember, arching the body speeds up the spin in the same manner that piking in the other direction does.

Proper Angle of Entry

The angle of entry is vertical, differing from the front dive layout. The entry line must conform to the path the center of gravity takes and allow for the backward movement of the body (which makes a slightly short entry appear very short).

Points To Remember

1. As the board is pressed, keep the head and shoulders over the board.

2. *Press forward* hard as the board lifts you.

3. Get into the swan *quickly* and hold it until the correct entry angle is reached.

15.3
Correct position in the air for the inward dive layout. (Ken Sitzberger is diver.)

15.3

The inward group of optional dives may be done using a tuck or a pike position and (very rarely) a flying position. These positions are identical with the ones used in the forward spinning group of dives.

Height of Board: Up to one-and-a-half somersaults may be done from the one- or three-meter boards. Doubles and two-and-a-half somersaults inward are used only from the three-meter board at the present time. The mechanics of spinning are the same for both boards.

Movement of Body During Inward Spins: Because the body moves forward in forward spinning dives, entries should be short of vertical. However, in inward spinning dives the body moves backward; therefore, entries must be vertical or nearly so. This is the major difference between the two groups of dives once the diver is in the air.

Mechanics of the Dives

The mechanics for all inward dives, except the inward dive layout, is the same. However, as the spin requirements of the dives increase (more angular momentum needed), the diver must push forward more vigorously and bring the upper body down farther, harder, and faster during the takeoff.

Overcoming Fear of the Board: Coaches should be aware that a major difficulty for inward dives is overcoming the fear of the board. The student must be made aware that the probability of hitting the board in this group of dives is no greater than in any other, if there is a proper takeoff. To be "safe," it doesn't matter what part of the body moves back as long as the center of gravity moves away from the board (as long as there is *some* lean).

If, in leaning, the head and shoulders move back, then there is great difficulty starting an adequate inward spin, although it will be simple to move away from the board. However, by moving the *hips back* and not the shoulders, the diver accomplishes exactly what he wants: his weight is moving back away from the board, while his head and shoulders remain over the board in a good position to start down vigorously. (16.1) Notice that the head is moving down directly over the board and the hips have moved well back.

16.1
Proper start for inward spin.

Inward Somersault Tuck

This dive (16.2) is generally used only from the one-meter board. It is easy for the beginning competitor to learn.

Directions to the Diver

As the board lifts, lower the head and arms, straighten the legs, and push *forward*. Lift the hips and upper back (round-shouldered style) and spin under the lifting hips to a tight tuck.

After the somersault, kick the legs down and lift the head and chest for a vertical entry.

Points To Remember

1. Use a sit-back lean and a round-shouldered lift of the upper back for more lift (emphasis is on *less spin, more* lift).

2. Play the entry straight up and down.

16.2
Inward somersault tuck.

16.3

Inward One-and-a-Half Somersault Tuck

Directions to the Diver
As the board lifts, press down and *forward* and, at the same time, move the head and arms down directly—never try to lift the head. (16.3)

Spin under the lifting hips into a tight tuck. The tighter the tuck, the faster the spin. After one somersault *look for the water;* learn to see it. Kick the legs up and move the arms down and forward, stretching for a vertical entry.

Points To Remember
1. Never move the head and shoulders back on the takeoff.

2. *Always* start into the spin *immediately*— before the feet leave the board. If you lift the upper body and then bring it down after you are in the air, you will get stuck.

Inward Two-and-a-Half Somersault Tuck (Three-Meter Dive)

Directions to the Diver
Make sure to *move the hips back* while the board is pressed in order to get the necessary and correct kind of lean. As the board lifts, move the arms and head quickly *down* and push *forward* (toward the back end of the board). Think of lifting only the hips. *Never* make any effort to lift the head on the takeoff. (16.4)

As soon as you are in the air, tuck. When you *see* (and/or feel) that you are in the correct entry position, snap the legs up and move the arms forward. See the water and enter vertically as in the inward one-and-a-half somersault.

Starting the Spin from the Board: If the correct takeoff procedure is used, adequate lift will result. Don't try to get lift by lifting the upper body. Get the arms and head moving down and lift the hips—fast.

Points To Remember
1. Don't lift the head.
2. Start the spin as the board lifts.
3. Squeeze the tuck tightly.
4. The save is very effective for this dive and often necessary since so much spin must be started from the board.

Inward Spinning Pike Dives

The mechanics of spinning inward are similar whether the position is pike or tuck. The major difference is that for a given takeoff (the same angular momentum) a diver can spin much faster in the tuck position than he can in the pike.

Therefore, more angular momentum (more initial spin) must be started from the board for a pike dive than would be needed for the same dive when the tuck position is used.

16.3
Inward one-and-a-half tuck. Lower the head *before* leaving the board.
16.4
Inward two-and-a-half tuck.

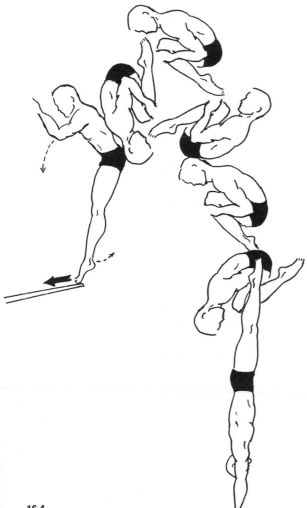

16.4

Inward Somersault Pike

Although this dive is listed from both the one- and three-meter board, I have never seen it used as a high dive. (16.5)

Directions to the Diver

As the board rises, start the head and arms down and lift the hips and back as the legs are extended. *Do all this before you leave the board.*

Move quickly into a tight closed-pike position, arms bent at right angles and pressed to the body, and the head as close to the knees as possible.

For the entry, drop the legs down out of the pike, sliding the hands along the thighs until the body is straight. Try for a vertical entry.

Inward One-and-a-Half Somersault Pike

At one time, this dive was considered impossible to do from the one-meter board. However, improvements in modern diving boards have made it a standard optional dive in men's competition, and now *girls* do it.

Directions to the Diver

Use the sit-back lean. As the board lifts, press (toward the back end of the board) and at the same time lower the upper body—head and arms—spinning under the lifting hips into a tight pike. (16.6) Catch the legs behind the knees, arms bent at right angles and pressed to the body. Squeeze the pike.

When one and a quarter somersaults are complete, you should *see the water*. Move the legs up and out of the pike and the arms down and *forward* to line up the body for the entry.

Points To Remember

1. Do not lean the shoulders back.

2. Start down into the spin immediately—before the feet have left the board.

3. Never lift the head on the takeoff.

4. Play the entry straight up and down. A short dive inward looks very short because the body is moving back away from the board during the entry.

5. Don't be afraid to roll the entry from the one-meter board. So much spin must be started that it is difficult to stop.

16.5
Inward somersault pike.

16.5

16.6
Inward one-and-a-half pike.

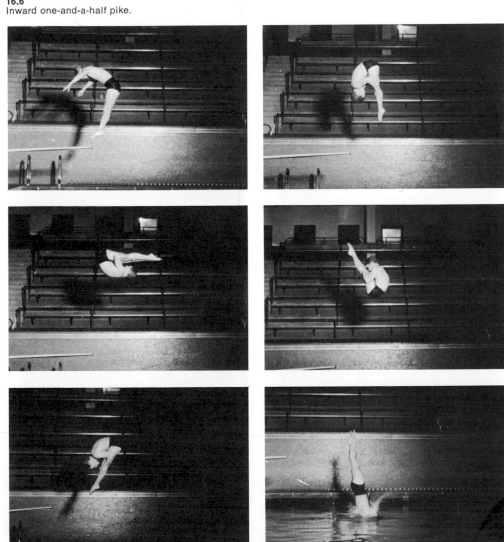

17.1a

A twisting dive is one in which the body makes at least one half turn on the long axis. It offers enormous variety in combination with all the other groups: one, two, and even three twists combined with anywhere from one half to two and a half somersaults.

At recent championships divers have used a triple twisting forward one-and-a-half somersault, a double twisting inward one-and-a-half somersault, a two-and-a-half twisting reverse one-and-a-half, and a full twisting two-and-a-half, all in the free position. The free position allows for combinations of tuck, pike, and layout. Since most of the twisting dives were using combinations of two positions, the added free position legalizes in the rules what has been in practice for many years.

Methods of Twisting
There are many ways to start twist in a dive. Often more than one method is acceptable for a particular dive. Frequently combinations of twisting techniques are employed in a single dive. A diver may twist by twisting from the board, using an action-reaction twist in the air, twisting out of a pike or out of an arch, combining any of the three previous methods.

Twisting from the Board
Twisting dives are often begun from the board, and the half twist and the full twist layout are almost always started this way. The direction of the twist is opposite to the direction in which the feet push against the rising board on the takeoff. (17.1)

17.1
The twist usually starts from the board in a half twist layout.

17.1 b

17.2 a   b   c   d

17.3

Trying a Twisting Jump from the Ground: For the moment forget diving and think of what you would do to twist a quarter or half turn in the air when jumping from the ground. The upper body turns in the direction of the twist as the feet push in the *opposite direction* against the ground. Do this a few times, and you'll feel that the feet push sideways as well as down. If you want to turn to the right, twist the trunk to the right and push to the left against the ground. Pushing in one direction, according to Newton's third law, causes a reactive push against the feet in the opposite direction, introducing a torque and causing twist around the long body axis. Exactly the same thing happens when a diver twists from the board. In a half twist layout the feet push diagonally forward to initiate twist (and spin), and the upper body leads the twist in the opposite direction. (17.2a) For a half twisting reverse dive the same thing happens when the feet push diagonally back. (17.2b)

This principle also applies on back takeoffs. For an inward dive layout with one half twist, the feet would push diagonally forward (17.2c), and for a back dive layout with a half twist, the feet would push diagonally backward with the upper body leading the twist in the opposite direction. (17.2d)

Action-Reaction Twist

When a body is free in space, movement of a part of it in one direction results in movement by the rest of that body in the opposite direction. This principle has been applied to the training of astronauts. The weightlessness they will experience outside the earth's gravitational field has necessitated special instruction in action-reaction body movements. For example, if a weightless astronaut tries to turn a bolt with a wrench, he will rotate one way as the bolt turns the other. If he lifts his legs, his upper body will move down. If he lowers his arms, his body moves up. Moving his arms across his chest in one direction will twist his body in the opposite. This is the principle of the action-reaction twist. (17.3) It is limited, since no angular momentum is introduced, and once the arms have stopped moving, the twist stops. However, the twist can be continued by moving the arms across the body and then circling them down next to the body and *parallel* to the axis of rotation, followed by a repetition of this circular movement. Here again, should the arms stop moving, the twist will stop. Since dives occur in a limited time, this method of twisting is rarely satisfactory for more than a half twist.

A back dive or a reverse dive layout with one half twist can be done without leading the twist from the board, using the action-reaction method. The layout position is taken with no twist, and to twist the body to the right, the right arm is brought across the chest to the left side. Then, by circling the arm down close

17.2
The feet push diagonally opposite to the desired twist: (a) front dive with half twist; (b) reverse dive, half twist; (c) inward dive, half twist; (d) back dive, half twist.

17.3
Using an action-reaction twist; the diver's left arm is moving toward his right side resulting in the twist of his body toward his left.

to the body toward the water, the half twist is completed.

Circumduction: Another method of introducing an action-reaction twist is to circumduct part of the body in one direction to cause twist in the opposite direction.

Circumduction is the circling of one end of a long object while the other end remains still. For example, one end of a long stick is circled in the air while the other end rests on the ground.

When the arms, legs, or even one half of the body moves in this way in the air, the reaction twists the body in the opposite direction to the circumducting member.[1] A back dive with one half twist and a front jackknife with one half twist can be done using this method alone.

How Does a Cat Turn Over?

When a cat is dropped upside down and turns himself over to land on his feet, he is using the same technique a diver uses to twist in the action-reaction style. If the cat twists his upper body around, then according to the action-reaction principle the lower body will twist in the opposite direction, and he'll go nowhere. Therefore, he instinctively varies the moments of inertia of his front and rear legs to his advantage as follows: The cat first extends his rear legs and circles them rapidly backward into an arched body position. As the legs are whipped back, they also *circumduct* in a direction opposite to the desired twist. The upper body is turned, twisting against the force of the circumducting and extended legs. When the legs are extended, they have a large moment of inertia, and it requires a large force to cause them to rotate. A simple way of saying this is that they resist turning. A tightrope walker uses a long balancing pole for the same reason. The pole has a large moment of inertia due to its length. It takes a large force to turn it. The performer can push against the pole (it resists turning) to help keep his balance, as though he were leaning against a solid rail.

As the cat's upper body moves back away from the fully extended and circumducting legs, his front legs are tucked in close to his body, giving them a small moment of inertia and enabling them to be turned against the large moment of inertia of his rear legs, and though the twisting forces will be equal in both directions, the upper half of his body will turn farther than the lower half. He pushes against the lower extended legs, which resist turning just as the tightrope walker pushes against the balancing pole.

When the cat's upper half is face down with the body in an arched position, he extends the front legs (increasing their moment of inertia) and at the same time circumducts them. The result is that the lower half of the body turns in the opposite direction to finish the twist. As this final step occurs, the rear legs are tucked in close to the body (decreasing their moment of inertia), and the cat lands on his feet.

During a dive, when the diver circumducts his arms or legs, he twists exactly as the cat did when it turned itself over.

Twisting out of a Pike or an Arch

A third way of twisting is a complicated method but one that enables somersaults and twist to be combined most efficiently. It is complicated because not only does it introduce new methods of twisting but it incorporates the two previously discussed methods as well: twisting from the board and action-reaction twisting.

Speeding Up Twist from the Board: If a spinning dive starts with some twist from the board, bringing the arms close to the body and opening the pike or straightening the arch speeds up the twist (by moving the body mass closer to the twisting axis). Regardless of *how* the arms are moved close, the speed of the twist will increase. However, if this is done in a particular way, it will introduce an additional and *essential* twisting force.

Tipping the Body off the Spinning Axis: The arms are more effective when they move in an arc parallel to the twisting axis. Starting with the arms at right angles to the body in open-pike position, one arm moves side-up above the head, and the other side-down to the final position against the body, rather than forward and back. (17.4)

When a body is turning around an axis in space, it has and will continue to have angular momentum. If the body is tilted sideways off axis (by the arms), a twisting force is developed as well. *Every time a diver does a somersault with a twist, the body tilts sideways.* The tilting is again due to the third law, since when one arm is raised side-up above the head and the other lowered side-down, the body turns sideways in the direction opposite to the way the arms were circled.

Facing the diver, if he raises his right arm and lowers his left, you will see his body turn sideways, as in a cartwheel, toward his left side. When this is done while spinning on a lateral axis (spinning forward, reverse, inward, or back), a force for twisting toward the raised arm will develop, and the diver will continue to twist as long as he maintains this position. Because angular momentum is conserved, the speed of the twist will be proportional to the speed of the spin, so that in a full twisting one-and-a-half somersault using this method, the faster the forward spin started from the board, the faster the twist will be. This is an interesting fact, and every good diver knows this instinctively. (See Chapter 19, Optional Twisting Dives.)

17.4
In spinning-twisting dives the arms are moved to the body one up and one down rather than forward and back.

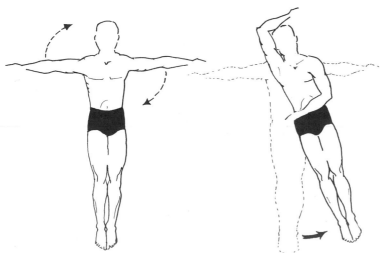

17.4

Speeding Up the Twist: Remember that the speed of the twist will increase when the body is straightened from either an arch or a pike position. To understand why this is true, keep in mind the principle that there is an imaginary axle around which the body is turning and that this "axle" goes through the top of the head and comes out through the toes.

A body that is straight along this axis will be twisting as fast as possible. Conversely, when the body is in open-pike position with the arms and legs extended at right angles to the twisting axis, the twist will be the slowest possible. (17.5)

There is strong evidence that the main source of twist in a dive comes from the sideways tipping of the body. When a spinning diver twists his upper body to the right in order to twist to the right, he causes his legs to move out of the pike to the left. This sideways tipping of the body is what really causes the twist to occur. (17.6) Although a diver thinks and feels that by twisting his head and trunk to the right he will twist to the right, this is true only under certain conditions and for an entirely different reason than he supposes.

There are two prerequisites essential to a successful twist: the body must be turning (angular momentum must be present), and the body must be tipped sideways from either a piked or arched position. If a diver jumped from a tower without twist or spin, with his body straight, he could *not* twist right by turning his upper body to the right. According to Newton's third law, as the trunk turned to the right, the legs would turn to the left, and no sustained twist would happen. If the diver was piked as he turned his upper trunk to the right, his legs would move over to the left; that is, he would tip sideways (action-reaction). But still no twist could occur because the second prerequisite—spin—was missing. Now, if he spins in a piked or arched position as he leaves the tower and then twists his trunk so that his legs move over, twist will occur because both requirements are satisfied: angular momentum is present, and the body is tipped sideways.

17.5
In the open-pike position the arms and legs are at right angles to the twisting axis.

17.6
Twisting the trunk to the right while in a pike position moves the legs to the left.

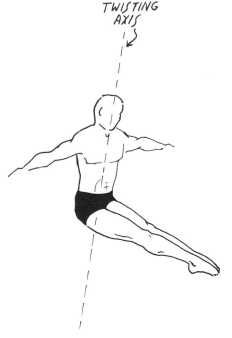

TWISTING AXIS

17.5

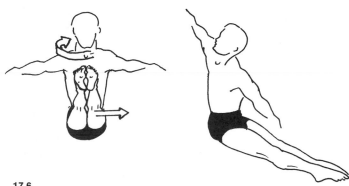

17.6

78   Asymmetric Body Position

An asymmetric body turning in space tends to twist as well as spin. Try throwing an object such as a claw hammer in the air so that it spins. Try to prevent it from twisting; it is almost impossible. Every time it is thrown, the hammer will twist at least one full turn.

Since the human body is not rigid and has the ability to change its shape, it can become unbalanced (by moving the arms, twisting the trunk, etc.), and twisting will be facilitated.

Combinations of the aforementioned styles of twisting are often used in a single dive. This is particularly true in a full, double, or triple twisting one-and-a-half somersault and will be explained in detail later on.

On a recent team trip I was discussing with the divers the reasons for circling the arms sideways for twist and how a fast twist results when the body is tipped off axis. I had a clear understanding of how this happened, and why, but because of a rather sketchy mathematics and physics background was unable to explain this phenomenon in mathematical terms. One of the M.I.T. varsity divers, Dixon Cleveland '68, agreed to write a brief paper explaining the mechanics of twisting in terms of vector analysis. The material in the Appendix was written by him, including the illustrations, and is reproduced here verbatim. It is clear, succinct, and easy to understand. If you are interested in really understanding what happens, read it. It certainly proves without a doubt that the tilting of the body in twisting dives is a definite aid to increasing the amount of twist and speeding up the twist.

[1]For example, if you were to jump off a bridge with one arm overhead, you could twist like a dervish by whirling that arm in a small circle above your head—or, in other words, circumducting that arm rapidly. If the arm circumducted clockwise, the body would twist counterclockwise, and vice versa.

Front Dive, Half Twist Layout

Although the half twist is an easy dive to learn, it is difficult to do well. (18.1, next page) The following directions are for a diver who twists toward his right side and are reversed for anyone twisting to the left.

Directions to the Diver

Establish the forward spin as for a front dive. At the same time *lead the twist from the board* in the same way that you would do a jump with a quarter turn from the ground—by pushing sideways with your feet. Twist with your feet, not with your arms which stay in swan position. (18.2) Look at the water over the left shoulder and enter as a back dive layout. However, try to think of the dive as a front dive turning to another front dive toward the board rather than as a front dive turning to a back dive.

Mechanics of the Dive

Controlling a half twist depends largely on what a diver does as he leaves the board. Once he is in the air, the diver is limited in the corrections he can make because of the required layout position; only minor changes of the position of the arms and the amount of body arch can be used to control the forward spin or the twist. Hence an accurate amount of twist and spin should be started from the board.

18.2
The correct body position of the half twist layout.

18.1
Half twist layout. Note that during the takeoff into the dive the twist has definitely started before the feet have left the board. During the stretch for the entry the head is in front-dive position. (Diver is Holt Maness.)

Starting the Twist by the Push of the Feet: If the twist is to be toward the right side, the push of the feet on the takeoff must be *diagonally* to the left with the upper body turning to the right. This is the major source of twisting. There is no doubt that twist can occur in the air by use of an action-reaction twist (moving the arms one way and twisting the body in the opposite direction). However, the style of the dive would be inferior.

Controlling the Spin in the Air: If necessary, to speed up the spin in the air, the diver can increase the body arch and move the arms down to shorten the radius of gyration. Conversely, too much forward spin can be corrected by eliminating the arch and moving the hands together overhead.

Correcting the Twist: If the diver starts with insufficient twist from the board, he can increase it by pressing the body away from the leading arm. If the left arm is moved in a direction opposite to the twist (toward the left), a force will move the body away from the arm (to the right). However, the smoothness of execution will be affected. Every effort should be made to leave the board with the proper forward spin and twist so that such corrections are unnecessary.

Stopping the Twist: You can slow down twist by increasing the body arch and spreading the arms to swan position at the peak of the dive.

This position speeds up the forward spin and slows down the twist because the twisting radius is increased while the spinning radius is decreased.

Entry

Although the body enters the water in the position of the back dive layout, a diver finds it helpful to think of the dive as moving from a front dive to another front dive toward the board. This encourages him to keep his head in the proper position and to *see* the water from the top of the dive until the entry.

The angle of entry should be well short of vertical to conform with the path the center of gravity takes and to allow for the remaining spin. The dive always continues to turn underwater for a smooth, splash-free entry.

It seems considerably easier to do this dive if there is slightly more forward lean than is needed for a front dive without twist.

Points To Remember

1. Start the twist from the board by pushing sideways with your feet.

2. Look over the shoulder at the water from the top of the dive.

3. Arch the body and spread the arms to stop the twist.

4. *Look* at the water during the entry and continue to turn underwater as for a back dive.

Front Dive with Half Twist Pike

Because it is an extremely difficult dive to do well, the half twist, pike position (front jack-knife with a half twist) is rarely used by competitors.

Directions to the Diver

Move into a jackknife position early on the way up. (18.3) Then, while the legs move out of the pike, look forward and twist the trunk away from the legs. When the body is fully extended, continue into a slightly arched position. See the water again and enter as in a layout half twist.

Mechanics of the Dive

The dive begins with no lead of the twist, no rushing into the pike position, eyes on the water.

The twisting action used—circumduction—imitates the manner in which a cat flips over. (See Chapter 17, Twisting Dives: General Principles.)

If the arms are extended and circumducted in one direction, the body will twist in the opposite direction. In my opinion, this is used considerably more than many people realize in all twisting dives. For example, a back dive with a half twist can be done using *only* this to twist, as can a reverse dive half twist, and even a full twist layout.

The arm action also causes a slight sideways movement of the body as in a cartwheel. When the body is tipped off its forward spinning axis in this way, a force for twisting will develop which is proportional to the forward spin. This will be very small, since there is so little forward spin to begin with.

Slowing Down the Spin and Stopping the Twist: When the body is straightened out of the pike position, the forward spin slows down. Since there was no angular momentum around the twisting axis to begin with, the twist will stop when the body is realigned, after the half twist is completed.

The Entry

The entry line is always slightly short of vertical. But here again the diver *thinks* of the entry as a front dive toward the board.

Points To Remember

1. Always start as an ordinary front dive pike—with no twist.

2. After the touch circumduct the arms and legs in the direction opposite to the desired twist.

3. Proceed as in a half twist layout.

4. *See* the water before the entry.

18.3
Half twist pike. Beautiful jackknife position and a perfect entry. (Diver is Frank Manheim.)

18.3

Back Dive or Reverse Dive Layout with One Half Twist

Both of these dives are attractive and simple to learn. Once the diver is in the air and spinning, the mechanics of twisting are identical. The differences in the two dives are in the methods of starting the spin and in the angle of entry.

Directions to the Diver

Lead the twist slightly from the board. *Do not look back.*

Take the layout position and, to twist to the left, bring the left arm toward the right and across the chest and the right arm up close to the head. At the same time, turn the head to the left to *see* the water. (19.1) Continue to circle the left arm close to the body and down.

For the entry the back dive is slightly short, and the reverse dive is vertical.

Mechanics of the Dives

Keeping the Head in Line: In neither twisting dive is the head rotated back, as for the dive without twist; it is kept in line with the body. This position makes it easier to twist since the head is along the twisting axis. When the head is back, it has moved away from the axis and slows the twist considerably.

Twisting: There are two acceptable styles of executing these dives. In one the layout position is held *before* the twist, and in the other it is held *afterward.*

There are several things a diver does to help himself twist. He twists from the board; he uses the arms in an action-reaction manner; and he circumducts the arms. The method described in the Directions to the Diver depends on action-reaction twist and holds either a back or reverse layout position *before* twisting. A second workable method depends on the circumduction of one arm and holds a swan position after the twist.

In the second method the diver leaves the board with the upper body turning in the direction of the desired twist (toward his left side). On the way up, the left arm circumducts (in the opposite direction to the desired twist),[1] and then both arms move out to the side into a swan position, when the half twist is completed. This arm action not only accomplishes the twist but stops it as well, when the arms are spread out.

Points To Remember

1. Keep the head in line—don't look back at the start.

2. Lead the twist from the board slightly.

3. Bring the arm across opposite to the direction of the desired twist (or circumduct one arm).

4. See the water; look for it from the top of the dive.

19.1
Reverse dive with half twist; the diver uses the action-reaction twist.

Full Twist Layout

In this dive assume that the twist will be toward the diver's right side. If the twist is to be toward the left, the twisting procedure is reversed.

Directions to the Diver

Leave the board as for a front dive layout, leading the twist *slightly* from the board. Look at the water. (19.2) Hold the layout position and, just before the peak of the lift, bring the arms close to the body quickly (near the head) and turn the head sharply, looking over the right shoulder to *see the water again.* You see the water twice, once on the way up and again after completing half of the twist.

Continue moving the right arm to the left, circling it down, close to the body, toward the water for the entry. The entry is as for a front dive layout.

Mechanics of the Dive

A full twist layout requires a diver to establish forward spin possible in the air since the lay-the board. There are limited adjustments of the forward spin possible in the air, since the layout position must be maintained. Tucking or piking to increase the speed of the spin are unacceptable.

Starting the Twist from the Board: The twist is *led from the board* by twisting the upper body slightly to the right and by pushing the feet down and *diagonally* forward toward the left corner of the lifting board.

On the way up the diver is in a position comparable to a front dive layout, arms above the head, eyes on the water, and the body turning very slightly on the long axis (twisting).

Speeding Up the Twist: Just before reaching the peak of the lift, when the arms are brought close to the body, the small amount of twist started from the board speeds up. (The moment of inertia decreases around the long axis and, to conserve angular momentum, the twist speeds up.) This is exactly what the ice skater does to speed up the turning of the body.

Seeing the Water Twice: To perform a full twist, the head must make a full rotation. Therefore, the eyes cannot be kept on the water all the time for a successful dive.

When the arms move in to speed up the twist, the head is turned quickly to the right. This fully rotated position of the head enables the diver to see the water again, long before his body has completed the twist, and is very useful in helping to control the dive.

Using an Action-Reaction Twist: When the arms move in, the right arm is actually circled from the side-out position to the left. The twist increases while the arm is moving because of the action-reaction principle; the body twists to the left as the arm moves to the right.

Finally, during the drop the right arm continues its circular movement down toward the water and *away* from the body (toward the right). This final movement of the right arm helps to stop the twist since there is a force against the body in the opposite direction; Newton's third law. The arm moving to the right twists the body to the left or cancels the twist.

One sees this movement of checking twist in many of the twisting dives: at the end of a full twisting one-and-a-half somersault and in the back and reverse one-and-a-half twisting somersault dives as well.

Points To Remember

1. Lead the twist from the board *slightly*. Don't overdo the twisting from the board—it becomes difficult to stop.

2. See the water twice: once as the dive moves up and again after the body has twisted half way. This gives you good control.

3. Bring the arms in to speed up the twist just *before* reaching the peak of the lift.

4. Use the right arm to finish and to stop the twist by moving it close to the body and then down toward the water.

19.2
Full twist layout. Arms are brought in to speed up
twist while the head is turned sharply to see the
water again.

a

b

d

e

g

h

j

k

m

n

c

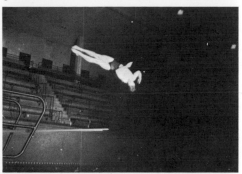

f

i

l

19.3
Full twisting one-and-a-half. The forward somersault starts from the board with a sharp pike. To twist, the arms move side-up and side-down to the body as the pike is eliminated.

Full Twisting, Double Twisting, and Triple Twisting One-and-a-Half Somersaults; Free Position

The full twisting, double twisting, and triple twisting one-and-a-half somersaults forward are done in the same way. The major difference is that a greater *forward* spinning force (and twisting force) must be started as the number of twists increases. There are two reasons why this is so: (1) as more twists are done, the layout position (in which the diver twists) must be held for the additional time needed, which slows down the forward spin for a longer time; and (2) the faster the forward spin, the faster the twist. (See Chapter 17, Twisting Dives: General Principles.)

Directions to the Diver
While the board is lifting, lower the head and lift the hips *immediately*. (19.3c) At the same time press down and *forward* with the feet. *Never* lift the head.

Leave the board with the arms in open-pike position. As soon as the feet are in the air, (1) kick the legs up and out of the pike, (2) twist the trunk to the right, and (3) bring the arms close to the body. All this happens simultaneously. (19.3d, e, k)

The method of bringing the arms to the body is important. Bring the arms to the body by circling the right arm side-up over the head and the left arm side-town and across the chest (not forward and backward). (This was clearly illustrated in Chapter 17.)

After the twists are completed, pike back toward the legs and move the arms to open-pike position again. (19.3j) See the water. Enter as in a forward one-and-a-half somersault pike.

Mechanics of the Dives
These dives involve a highly complex series of movements: establishing, slowing down, and speeding up of the forward spin; transferring the forward spinning momentum to twisting momentum; starting and stopping the twist.

Developing the Forward Spin: The forward spin starts in the same way as in all forward spinning dives.

Since it is impossible to establish spin (angular momentum) after you are in the air, everything that causes spin must occur before the feet leave the board. Therefore the head should *never* be lifted on the takeoff. There should be no concern with getting lift because you will get enough lift if the dive is started properly, hips up and head down.

Twisting: There are many variations of style in executing a full twisting one-and-a-half somersault. Technically, no one style is more, or less, correct than the other. However, good style, in the sense of a more pleasing dive, involves an early twist in the layout position. Competent execution of a double or triple twisting one-and-a-half somersault *demands* this. (19.4)

The spectacular style that will be described and analyzed here was developed by Earl Clark, one of Ohio State University's diving greats. He originated the technique of an early twist (before more than half a somersault is completed), followed by a return to the pike position for the last part of the somersault.

88

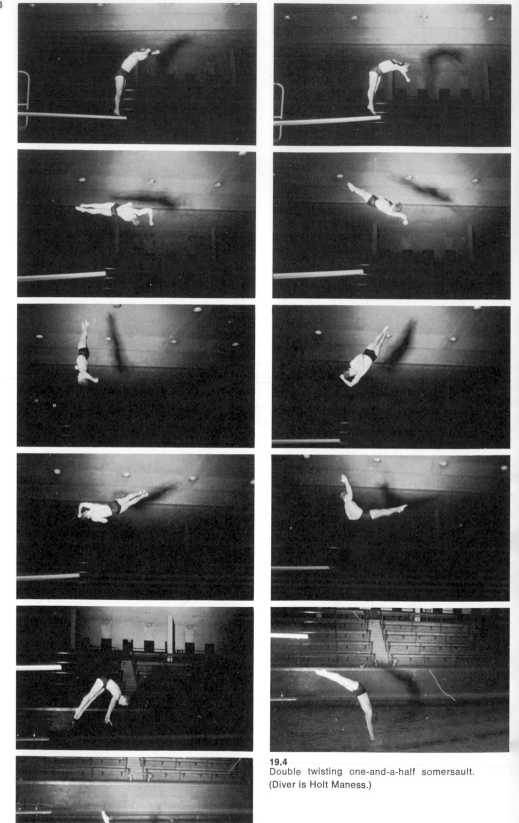

19.4
Double twisting one-and-a-half somersault.
(Diver is Holt Maness.)

There are at least three things a diver does to twist in these dives:

1. *He Twists from the Board:* A careful study of motion pictures reveals that the twist is often started from the diving board.

If the diver leaves the board in a pike position with some twist and then brings his arms close to the body as he straightens out of the pike, the speed of the twist will increase considerably. Again this is exactly what a pivoting ice skater does to speed up—brings the arms close to the body.

2. *He Twists Coming out of the Pike Position:* (19.5) Effective twist will occur only if the diver starts the twist *as* he straightens out of the pike.

3. *He Tips His Body off the Spinning Axis:* By circling the arms as described, side-up and side-down rather than forward and back as the pike is opened, the body rotates in the opposite direction (Newton's third law). For example, facing the diver head on, if his arms circle clockwise, his body will turn counterclockwise in the air (a cartwheel kind of turning).

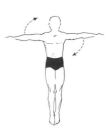

When a spinning body is moved off axis in this manner, twisting force is developed, and the farther the body is tipped, the faster the twist. For this reason the straight arms are circled and then bent at the elbows to continue the circling movement for maximum tipping of the body.

The resulting twisting force is directly proportional to the forward spinning speed, so that a diver who develops a larger amount of forward spin (angular momentum) from the board will twist faster when he circles the arms to the body.

Twisting Early
It is logical that a diver should begin his twist as soon as his forward spin is established, that is, as soon as his feet leave the board.

The sooner he starts, the sooner in the dive the twists are completed, enabling him to finish early and giving him the desired long drop to the water for the entry.

Slowing Down the Spin To Twist
When the legs are moved out of the pike and the body lengthened, the forward spin is slowed down considerably (just as it slows down when the body is stretched for the entry). This creates a spectacular twisting style because the diver seems poised in mid-air, twisting but not spinning forward. Of course, he is spinning forward somewhat, since the forward spin can never be completely stopped. The angular momentum forward is conserved throughout the dive, and only the *speed* of the spin can be varied.

Since the straightened body has the smallest moment of inertia around the long body axis, the twist will be the fastest possible in this position.

Resuming the Spin and Stopping the Twist for the Entry

At the completion of the twists, resumption of an open-pike position will start the diver spinning forward as rapidly as when he started the dive and will also stop the twist. With the open-pike position the weight moves closer to the lateral spinning axis, and the legs and arms are extended at right angles to the twisting axis. Therefore, the moment of inertia has increased around the long body axis and decreased around the lateral axis; to conserve angular momentum, the spin will speed up, and the twist will stop. The entry is exactly the same as for a forward one-and-a-half somersault pike.

Remember—whether the dive is to have one, two, or three twists, the important thing is to start the dive with more forward spin (angular momentum) as the number of twists increases.

Points To Remember

1. *Always* move the head and arms down immediately—as the board is lifting. Never lift the head at the start of these dives.

2. Start the twist early—snap the legs up and out of the pike and bring the arms side-up and side-down to the body. Do not move the arms forward and back.

3. Keep the arms as close to the body as possible during the twist and keep the body straight for maximum speed of twist.

4. As the number of twists increases, start a faster spin from the board.

5. Complete the twist(s) before piking again.

6. The forward (roll) save is quite effective for these dives, particularly from the one-meter board.

19.5

A series of photos showing parts of a full twisting one-and-a-half. Excellent arm and body position to twist. Note tilting of the body toward the diver's right side and the open-pike position to stop the twist. (Diver is Fletcher Gilders.)

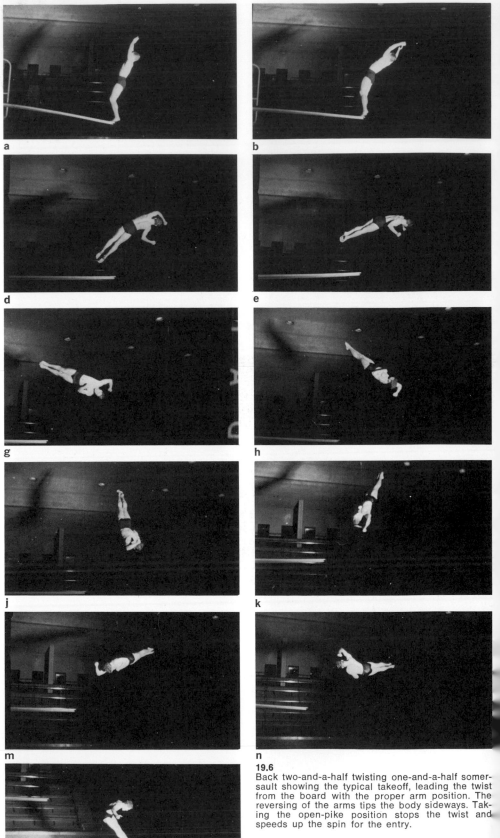

19.6
Back two-and-a-half twisting one-and-a-half somersault showing the typical takeoff, leading the twist from the board with the proper arm position. The reversing of the arms tips the body sideways. Taking the open-pike position stops the twist and speeds up the spin for the entry.

c

f

i

l

o

Back One-and-a-Half and Two-and-a-Half Twisting One-and-a-Half Somersaults; Free Position

Twisting is mechanically the same for forward or backward spinning dives. And in backward spinning dives the technique is the same for both one-and-a-half and two-and-a-half twists. Therefore, from the mechanical point of view the dives may be discussed together.

Directions to the Diver

Twist from the board and at the same time arch and reach back. If you twist to your right, your right arm must reach back and down toward the water and the left arm up and back over the head. (19.6b, c)

After completing one quarter to one half twist, snap the leading (lowered) arm side-up over the head and the other arm side-down and across the chest. At the same time eliminate the arch and twist the trunk toward the lifting arm. (19.6d, e, f) After completing the twist, sit into a deep open-pike position, spot the water, and enter exactly as for a forward one-and-a-half somersault pike. (19.6o, p)

If you follow these steps, you will actually do one half twist from the board, which will lead you into a forward full twisting one-and-a-half somersault.

Mechanics of the Dive

The diver gets his spin in this dive in the same way he gets it for any other back spinning dive: by circling and lifting the arms, arching and reaching back, and pressing back with the feet.

94

Starting the Twist: As explained in the general principles of twisting, there are several ways of initiating twist in a dive. In this dive, twist is initiated by (1) leading the twist from the board (19.7); (2) bringing the arms closer to the body and eliminating the arch (thereby decreasing the moment of inertia of the twisting body); (3) moving the body off its lateral spinning axis—tilting it.

Speeding Up the Twist: Shortly after the feet leave the board, the body arch should be eliminated and the arms brought close. This action will speed up the twist (which was started from the board) by shortening the radius of gyration around the long axis.

After the first one half twist, the dive is executed as a forward full twisting one-and-a-half: the arms do not move forward and back, they move side-up and side-down. Consequently the body is tipped sideways off its transverse spinning axis (cartwheel style); this action results in a twisting force in the direction of the lifted arm. This additional torque will be proportional to the amount of backward spin started from the board.

Stopping the Twist and Speeding Up the Spin: Straightening the body speeds up the twist and slows down the spin, resulting in the same spectacular twisting style as the full twisting one-and-a-half in which the body is poised in mid-air.

When the one-and-a-half or two-and-a-half twists are completed, it becomes necessary to stop the twist and speed up the spin again. Remember, the diver by his arm action had tilted his body sideways to add to the twist. By moving his arms out to the sides to open-pike position; that is, he moves his body back onto its lateral spinning axis. The open-pike position with the legs and arms extended away from the long body axis effectively stops the twist and increases the speed of the spin.

In addition, when the previously lifted arm moves out, it circles forward, around, and to the side in a direction exactly opposite to the direction of the twist. The result is a reactive force against the body that enables the diver to complete the twist and then stop it dramatically.

The Entry
Once the body is piked and spinning again, the dive proceeds as in a *forward* one-and-a-half somersault, open pike.

19.7
Start of a back twister from the one-meter board showing the twist from the board and the tilting of the body during the twist.

19.7

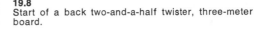

Differences Between the Two-and-a-Half and the One-and-a-Half Twisters

The back two-and-a-half twister needs more backward spin (angular momentum) and more twist started from the board than the one-and-a-half. These are the only major differences between the two dives, for the following reasons:

1. Because the body is in a straight (layout) position for a longer time in the two-and-a-half twister, the speed of the backward spin will be slowed down for a longer time.

2. The speed of the twist will be proportional to the initial spin from the board (the angular momentum).

3. If a greater twist momentum is started from the board, there will be a corresponding increase in the speed of the twist when the arms are brought close to the body.

Starting the Spin from the Board: The additional required spin is obtained by a more forceful takeoff into the dive; a harder press back (toward the water) with the feet; more rapid circling back of the arms during the press of the board; and a more distinct arching back on the takeoff. (19.8)

Points To Remember

1. Start the spin backward by arching back and reaching back with the arms.

2. Start the twist from the board by reaching one arm up overhead and the other down— turn sideways toward the lowered arm.

3. As soon as the feet leave, eliminate the arch and bring the higher arm rapidly down across the chest and the lower arm side-up overhead. Twist toward the lifting arm.

4. Sit into a deep open-pike position to stop the twist and to speed up the spin.

19.8
Start of a back two-and-a-half twister, three-meter board.

19.8

Reverse One-and-a-Half Somersault with One-and-a-Half Twists; Free Position

Once a diver has left the board and established his reverse spin, the mechanics and technique of this dive are almost identical with the back one-and-a-half twisting one-and-a-half somersault. (19.9) Reread the description of that dive. The two differences between the reverse and back twisters are the manner of starting spin and the entry.

Starting the Reverse Spin

The reverse spin starts from the board as for the reverse somersault layout: circle the arms back, arch, and push back against the board. The twist also starts from the board. The feet push diagonally back against the board in a direction opposite to the desired twist, and the trunk twists in the direction opposite to the push of the feet.

Speeding Up the Twist

In the air, as the arch is eliminated, the leading (and lowered) arm moves side-up and the other arm side-down, tipping the body off axis and speeding up the twist considerably. After completing the twist and half of a somersault, a deep open-pike position is assumed which stops the twist and speeds up the spin. The entry proceeds as for the *inward* one-and-a-half somersault pike. The correct angle of entry is vertical.

Points To Remember

1. Always start the twist and spin from the board.

2. Eliminate the arch as the arms are moved to the body to speed up the twist.

3. After the twist is completed, take a deep open-pike position to stop the twist and increase the speed of the spin.

4. Enter vertically, as for an inward one-and-a-half.

Reverse One-and-a-Half Somersault with Two-and-a-Half Twists

More reverse spin is needed for this dive (greater angular momentum) than for the reverse one-and-a-half twister. The additional spinning force helps to increase the speed of the twist and make up for the added time that the diver will be in the layout position. Aside from this, the mechanics and technique of the two dives are identical. Remember, the more reverse spin, the faster the twist. Go after the spin; the twist will take care of itself.

[1]As seen from above looking down, the left arm circumducts above the head in a counterclockwise direction to turn the diver to his left. The right arm stays above the head in line with the twisting axis.

19.9
Reverse one-and-a-half somersault with one-and-a-half twists.

19.9

Entries into the water will vary a great deal
depending upon the dive. The initial spinning
force (angular momentum), the direction of the
spin, and the distance from the board are all
factors that can change an entry. (20.1)

20.1
The correct entry position for forward spinning
dives.

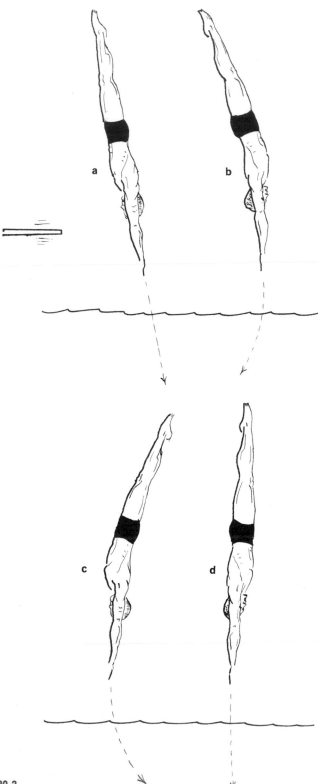

Conserving Angular Momentum: A crucial factor affecting entries is the fact that the spin of any dive can never be completely stopped. During the entry the body will always be turning, and the amount of spin left will depend on the angular momentum started from the board. Remember, angular momentum is always conserved. (See Chapter 1.) Even when the body is stretched out at its longest, arms overhead as for a head-first entry, which makes the slowest possible spin for a given dive, there will be *some* spin left, particularly in the multiple spinning dives.

Turning Underwater in the Direction of the Spin: For all entries, therefore, the body should continue to turn underwater in the direction of the spin, and the degree of turning will vary with the amount of spin left in the dive. For example, since a back two-and-a-half somersault starts with more initial spin (angular momentum) than a back dive, the body will turn more as it enters the water (toward the surface). The back-dive entry can be straighter down. This is clearly explained in Chapter 21, Saving Dives.

Varying the Angle of Entry with the Diving Groups: For all forward and backward spinning dives, the entry should be slightly short of vertical. (20.2a, b) For reverse and inward spinning dives the entry can be more nearly vertical. (20.2c, d) This is true of all feet-first entries as well. (20.3)

20.2
The correct entry angles for (a) forward spinning dives, (b) backward spinning dives, (c) reverse spinning dives, (d) inward spinning dives.

20.3
The correct entries for feet-first dives: (a) forward spinning, (b) reverse spinning, (c) back spinning, (d) inward spinning.

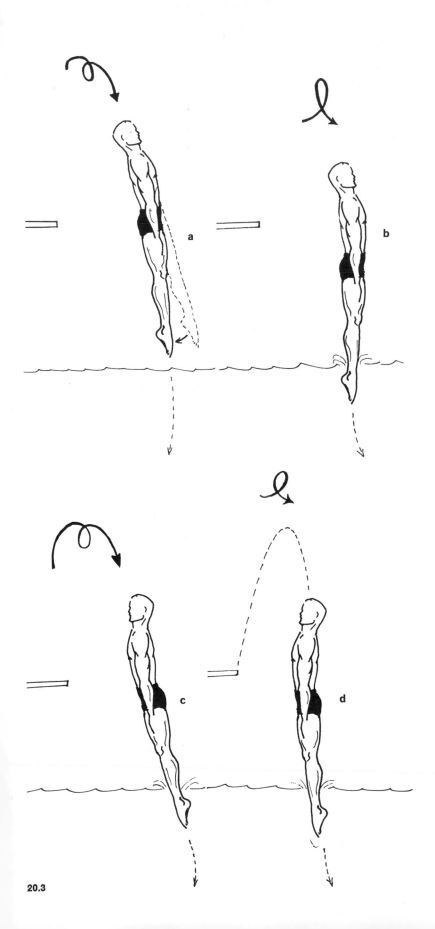

a

b

c

d

20.3

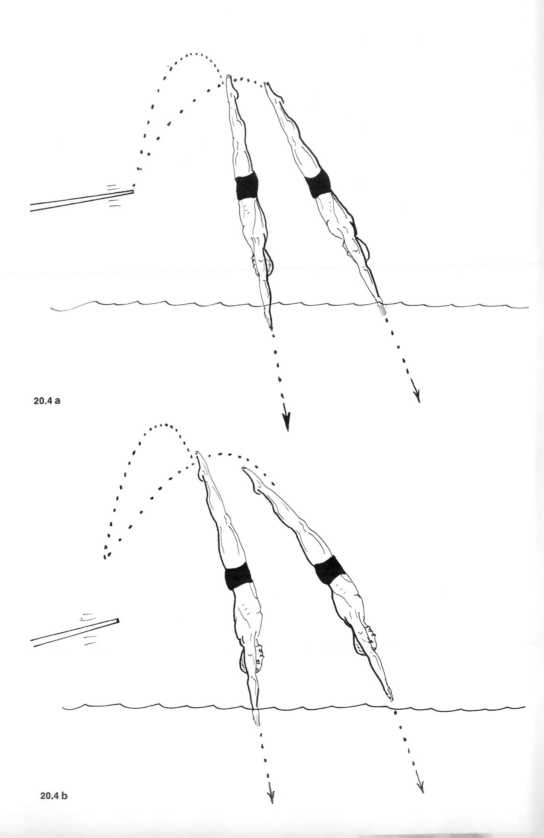

20.4 a

20.4 b

Lining Up the Entry with the Path of the Center of Gravity: For a perfect entry the line of the body as it enters the water should conform as closely as possible with this path while allowing for the remaining spin. Clearly then, the angle of entry, in addition to changing with different dives, will be affected by the distance from the board to the point of entry. The farther out the dive, the shorter the correct entry line of forward and backward spinning dives. (20.4) For inward and reverse dives the farther out the dive, the farther over the angle of entry must be.

Body Positions During Entries; Head-First Entries: For forward and inward spinning dives the arms are fully extended, the hands together overhead, the shoulders pressed against the ear, and the eyes looking at the water over the tops of the hands. The abdomen is flat, knees straight and legs together, the buttocks squeezed tightly, and the body in a straight line from the finger tips to the toes. For backward and reverse spinning dives the arms are fully extended and the hands together overhead. The body is slightly arched with the arch high in the chest (and *never* at the waist), the abdomen flat, buttocks squeezed tightly. The line of the body from the chest to the toes is straight. The diver should see the entry point on the water over the tops of his hands.

Feet-First Entries: For all feet-first entries the body is slightly arched, again using a high chest arch. The arms are straight and pressed against the sides, hands on the thighs (fingers straight and together). The head is in the natural position, eyes looking forward, and the body is at an "attention" position during the entry.

20.4
The angle of entry changes as the dive moves farther out.

102   **A New Entry Technique:** There is a new style of head-first entry that seems to have merit. Instead of entering with the hands together and finger tips pointed to the water, the hands are several inches apart with the fingers curved and spread and a flat-hand position, palms to the water. (20.5) The entry that results is almost completely without splash (if the body is close to being properly aligned). One hears, as well, a very interesting sound as the body moves through the surface of the water—similar to paper tearing—which, combined with the extraordinary softness of the entry, completes the illusion of the perfect entry.

Why there is no splash is a matter for conjecture. I have heard one theory that the hands punch a hole in the water which then rushes in to fill up the hole. This seems a bit farfetched. I rather believe it has to do with another phenomenon. The spread-finger, flat-hand position causes lots of air to be pushed down into the water. When observed from underwater, the amount of air bubbles is unusual. These numerous air bubbles affect the entry in two ways. First, in the manner of the aerated faucet a stream of air bubbles is introduced into the water. The mixture of air and water prevents splashing even when a pot or dish is put into the water stream. Similarly, the diver's body passes through the mixture of water and air bubbles without much splash. Second, a mass of air and water is easily compressible, whereas ordinary water is not. The spongy air-water "gives" as it is compressed by the returning water, and the resulting splashless boiling of the water is observed.

Tower divers doing feet-first dives first noticed that turning the feet up—flattening them—just as they hit the water causes the same phenomenon. The water seems to boil and bubble rather than splash, and there is the characteristic "tearing" sound. It was observation of these feet-first entries from the ten-meter tower that led to the development of the effective flat-handed entry. Experiment with it. If it works for you, use it.

20.5
The flat-hand-entry position of a back one-and-a-half tuck as demonstrated by Chuck Knorr.

Modern diving, with its emphasis on the vertical entry and the use of multiple spinning dives, makes saving dives a necessary part of the competitor's equipment. Dives can be saved in the air as well as during the entry into the water. Essentially, saving a dive refers to correcting errors in execution (too much or too little spin) and, also, to promoting the illusion of the vertical entry into the water when a dive is "long" or over. Despite arguments to the contrary, a degree of saving is necessary on *all* back spinning dives and on many of the forward spinning ones. Judicious use of saving techniques is the mark of a highly skilled performer.

Applicable Laws of Motion
There are some fundamental laws of motion that must be made clear to understand the mechanics of saving dives. These have been discussed earlier, but, reviewed briefly, they are the following:

Angular Momentum: The quantity, the amount of spin. This is conserved throughout the dive.

Angular Velocity: The speed, the revolutions per minute, of the spin. This can be changed by varying the moments of inertia of the parts of the body—by bringing the weight closer to the spinning axis to speed up the spin, and vice versa.

Newton's Third Law: The law of action-reaction. When a body is free in space, a movement by part of it in one direction results in a movement in the opposite direction and of equal force by the rest of the body. For example, when a diver pikes *after* he is in the air, his feet will move toward his hands, and his hands will move toward his feet.

104

Saving Dives in the Air

The basic principle of saving a dive in the air is the control of the speed of the spin: the slowing down or speeding up of the turning of the body. This is done by increasing or decreasing the moment of inertia of the body around its spinning axis. Since angular momentum is conserved, the closer the body weight is brought to the axis of rotation, the faster the spin, and vice versa. This is used by divers constantly.

Saving a "Short" Dive: A dive that is short is one in which there is not enough spin. A diver who realizes that he will be short on the spin of a back dive layout, for example, can speed up his spin by increasing the arch of his back (decreasing the moment of inertia). This is similar to piking in a forward spin. By piking, the diver speeds up his spin. Arching the back accomplishes the same thing, even though the body bends in the other direction. This is about all that can be done for a back dive that is short.

Saving a Dive That Is "Long" or Over: If the back dive is going over because the diver had developed too much spin from the board, he can slow down the speed of his spin by eliminating the arch of the body and extending his arms overhead to make himself as tall as possible (the moment of inertia increases). The same principle applies to the more complicated dives. After leaving the board for a one-and-one-half somersault, tuck position, a diver who realizes that he is spinning too slowly can stay in the tuck for as long a time as possible in order to continue spinning at maximum speed. Some divers will even spread the knees slightly and tuck the head between the knees, getting even closer to the center of gravity in order to spin faster. If the diver is spinning too fast, he comes out of the tuck sooner to lengthen the body in order to slow the spin down. The same thing is true for twisting dives. In a front dive with a full twist, for example, after the twist is started from the board, when the arms are brought closer to the body, the speed of the twist increases; when the arms extend away from the body, the twist slows down.

The principle of increasing and decreasing the velocity of the spin by changing the moment of inertia is clearly illustrated by the ice skater who spins on one skate with the arms out. As the arms are brought closer to the body, the spin gets faster and faster. When the arms are spread out, the spin slows down. This is one of the major ways that dives are controlled in the air.

21.1
Saving a dive. The principles of turning underwater in the direction of the spin for (a) back and reverse spinning dives, and (b) forward and inward spinning dives.

21.1

Saving Dives During the Entry into the Water

In considering that any dive is at least one half a somersault, a diver has some spin (angular momentum) when he leaves the board. Since angular momentum is conserved, and will continue unless an outside force is introduced, he will be spinning when his body hits the water.

Turning Underwater During the Entry: The principle of saving a dive during the entry is to continue to turn underwater *only* in the direction of the spin of the dive. (21.1) This enables the feet to enter the water in the same place on the surface as the hands.

The "Scooped" Save for Back Spinning Dives: The farther over the dive, the shallower the spin underwater. In severe cases in backward spinning dives, the knees *are allowed to bend* as the diver's legs pass through the water surface, giving the illusion of a vertical entry. (21.2) This, however, seems to happen naturally and should not be overdone.

Playing the Back Spins Slightly Over: On certain dives, such as a back one-and-one-half somersault layout, it's almost impossible to do the dive well without some saving technique during the entry. Most good divers will play all backward spinning dives slightly over, and then save if necessary. This gives a better-looking entry and is much the safer execution.

21.2
Back and reverse spinning dives. The farther over the dive, the shallower the scoop underwater.

21.2

Saving Forward Spinning Dives in the Air

In forward spinning dives the same principles apply. In a swan dive, for example, if the diver feels he will be short (not enough spin), then he can increase the arch in his back while in the air and remain arched until the correct entry position is reached. By so doing, he increases the speed of the spin, correcting the error. (21.3a)

If a dive appears to be going over (too much spin), he eliminates the arch and moves the arms forward until the body is as long as possible. This lengthens the radius of gyration (increasing the moment of inertia), slowing down the speed of the spin. (21.3b)

The "Roll" Save for Forward Spinning Dives:

During the entry of a forward spinning dive, such as a two-and-one-half somersault, by continuing to turn underwater in the direction of the spin, one can save a dive that is over. The diver rolls over into a jackknife position as he enters the water and finishes upside down, under the surface of the water. (21.4)

Also, by a greater or lesser degree of flexion at the hips, as the legs move through the water surface, the illusion of a vertical entry can be created. (21.4b)

Learning the Saves in Shallow Water

An excellent method of learning the underwater saves is to practice in shallow water, 3 to 4 feet deep. (21.5, 21.6) Do a handstand on the bottom, allow the legs to fall over in either direction, and release the hands by lifting the body up (push down against the bottom). Then, as the body sinks back down into the water, go through the movements of saving previously described. Have someone check to see if the legs appear to enter the water vertically. The identical movements occur in the regular save, only in faster sequence.

Action-Reaction Saves in the Air

It is obvious from the foregoing discussion that the arms play an important part in the saving of dives. By extending the arms overhead, the spin is slowed down; and when the arms are brought closer to the body, the spin speeds up. They can serve in another way. When they are circled in any direction in mid-air, there is exerted on the body a force that turns it in the opposite direction. This is due to the action-reaction principle, Newton's third law.

If a person were falling from a high tower, feet first with no spin, by circling the arms up in front of the body and back down and around behind the body continuously and rapidly, he could cause the body to turn forward and enter the water head first, although he would never develop a sustained spin. When the arms stopped circling, the body would stop turning.

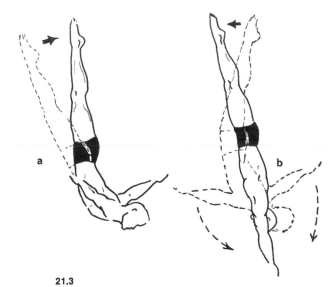

21.3

21.4

21.3
Increasing the arch speeds up the spin of layout dive. Lengthening the body slows the spin down.
21.4
The roll save for forward and inward spinning dives.
21.5
Learning the scoop-save technique in shallow water.
21.6
Learning the roll-save technique in shallow water.

21.5

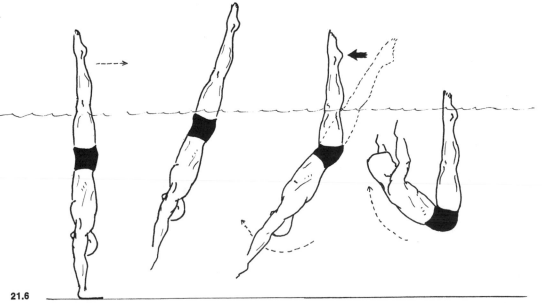

21.6

108 Circling the Arms To Save a Dive in the Air

As an example of this device used in a dive, one often sees a diver, when going over on a jackknife, circle the arms back, *up,* and around (clockwise, as observed from the right side of the diving board) after he touches his toes as he stretches for the entry. This slows down the spin during the time that the arms are circling.

In a similar manner, during a swan dive when a diver is short on the spin, he can circle the arms up, back, around, and down (counter-clockwise, seen from the right) as he reaches for the entry. (21.7) This speeds up the spin while the arms are cicling, causing the legs to go higher. This principle is used a great deal in all backward spinning dives. In a back one-and-one-half somersault tuck, for instance, after the diver kicks the legs out of the tuck and looks back for the water, he circles the arms back and, in so doing, holds the legs back.

Kicking into a Pike To Control Back Spinning Dives

When a diver comes out of a pike position, during the time the body is straightening away from the legs, there is exerted on the legs a force in the opposite direction that moves them back. This can be used to control tuck spinning dives as well as pike (reverse one-and-one-half somersault tuck) by kicking the legs out first into a pike position and then looking back for the entry. (21.8)

The use of this and the arm circling gives the diver three opportunities to correct or save the dive: (1) the opening of the pike; (2) the circling of the arms; (3) the underwater save, or pull.

Saves for Feet-First Entries

The rules state that the arms must be at the sides during feet-first entries into the water. Therefore, the amount of adjusting or saving that can be done in the air is limited (since the arms play such an important part in air saves). (21.9)

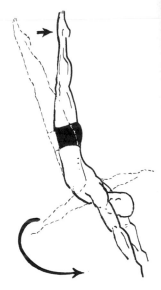

21.7
Action-reaction save in the air.

21.8
Controlling entries by piking out of spins.

21.9
Saving a front somersault with too much spin. By extending the body early, the spin is slowed down sufficiently for a perfect entry.

Playing Feet-First Entries Short: There is, however, one device used successfully by divers. By playing all forward spinning feet-first entries slightly short and then by increasing the amount of arch as needed, a diver can adjust the angle of entry if necessary. (21.10) (Since there should be some arch during the entry to conform with the correct entry path, this technique makes a lot of sense.)

Another reason to play feet-first entries short, is that when a feet-first dive is over, *it's over,* and that's about all there is to that. Just about the only effective thing that can be done to correct a feet-first dive that is *slightly* over is to split the legs, one forward and one back, just as they go beneath the surface of the water. This is not always successful. It is used on either forward or backward spinning dives as a last resort. Play *all* feet-first dives slightly short, then correct if necessary.

Saving dives is very much a part of modern diving. It is absolutely *essential* on some of the multiple spinning dives. Proper use of the save is the mark of the highly accomplished performer and takes great skill. It pays to practice and learn the different methods described in this chapter. After a while, saving becomes automatic. Without thinking about it, a diver will save when it's necessary.

21.10
Play all forward spinning feet-first dives slightly short. Then, by increasing the body arch as needed, line up for a proper entry.

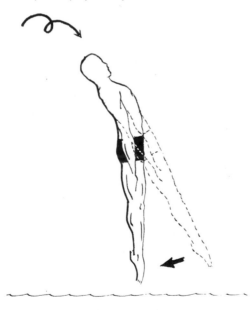

Fundamental Concepts

The purpose of this chapter is to give those with some knowledge of fancy diving a set of fundamental criteria that will help them to do an acceptable job of officiating:

1. See the dive as a whole unit, a complete picture, and not as a number of small unrelated parts.

2. When possible, grade on a scale comparative with all divers in the competition.

3. Deduct points when a diver misses a dive. Pay off for a good dive. In other words spread your scores—don't play safe.

Can the Grading Be Done for Parts of a Dive?

Theories have been advanced that a judge of diving should consider each part of the dive individually and then immediately arrive at a grade by a complex system of addition.[1] This seems very difficult, if not impossible.

The human mind cannot consider components of a movement that takes about 1.5 seconds, ascribe points to these parts, and finally, by adding the points together for a total score, arrive at a decision in two to three seconds.

Quick Impressions

Immediately preceding and during World War II, some excellent experimental work was done at Ohio State University in the Fine Arts Department relative to both art appreciation and aircraft recognition.

A silhouette of a plane was flashed for an instant on a screen, and the students learned to recognize and differentiate between American and enemy planes by observing these silhouettes as units. (This system is still in use by the Air Force today.) They did not concern themselves with details. There wasn't time.

When you look at a painting, you should see the whole picture, with each part related to every other part; you observe the painting as one complete unit, incidentally being composed of various parts. Children are now taught to read by recognizing groups of words, not each letter in each word. The same is true in learning to read music.

As a judge of diving, learn to see a dive as a complete unit, not as small disconnected parts. It is a matter of training. Get the whole picture. How did it impress you as a complete dive? Most good diving judges think of the grade immediately after a dive is done rather than dwell on a critical analysis of its good and bad points. However, if questioned, they can analyze what occurred in great detail. They retain an impression—the parts are there, but included in the general picture of the dive.

Comparative Scoring

In competition, when several divers are doing the same dives, the grades can be justified on a comparative basis. A full twisting one-and-a-half somersault done by two boys may be similar, but if one is better executed, is finished high, has a clean entry (thereby leaving the judge with a better impression of the dive, a better feeling if you will), it must on a comparative basis be given a higher score. Conversely, if the poorer dive follows the better one, the judge must give it a lower score.

Simply set your standard with the first dive you grade and make your scale of grading relative to that.

Spreading the Scores

A common error of inexperienced (and too often, experienced) officials of diving has been the tendency to "play it safe." By that, I mean to confine one's grades over a two- or three-point spread; for example, four to six points. When a diver does a good dive, he'll receive a grade of six; a really bad dive receives a four.

This is extremely unfair to a boy or girl who has done an excellent dive and is quite beneficial to the diver who misses. It is imperative that a missed dive be graded down in fairness to the other competitors. If this is not done, in a meet with two divers of comparable ability a missed dive does not penalize the diver sufficiently and, in a sense, keeps him in the running.

Spreading Grades when Warranted

Remember, always having the middle score is rarely the mark of a good diving judge. Use all the numbers when necessary.

Summary

1. Familiarize yourself with the diving rules and with diving in general. Know what a good dive looks like by watching good diving whenever possible. Study good diving films if they are available.

2. Learn to see the dive as a whole unit—not as unrelated parts. This takes a little experience and the proper state of mind. Get the impression.

3. When possible, grade on a comparative scale with all the divers in the competition.

4. Spread your scores; pay off for a good dive and grade down a poor one. Be courageous—don't play it safe.

[1]This is in compliance with the rule that stated "After each dive, . . . each judge . . . shall *immediately* and simultaneously flash his award."

References

Diving, Robert Clotworthy, Thomas Nelson & Sons, New York, 1962.
Springboard Diving, Phil Moriarty, The Ronald Press Co., New York, 1959.
Champions on Film (16mm diving film), Don Canham, 816 South State St., Ann Arbor, Mich.

A diver with no twist can develop twist by converting some of his spin. He can do this because of the law of conservation of angular momentum. Angular momentum can be represented graphically by a vector (arrow) **L**. Physically, the vector points in the direction of the axis of rotation:

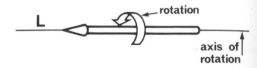

The law of conservation of angular momentum states that if no torques are applied to a body (which is the case for a diver who has left the board), the *total* angular momentum of the body will remain the same with respect to a stationary frame of reference.

The word *total* is a key point. It is often convenient to express a vector as the *sum* of some other vectors. In the following diagram, V_3 is the sum of V_1 and V_2:

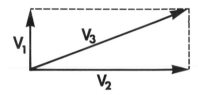

Thus if a body has two component vectors, V_1 and V_2, associated with it, the total vector of the body would be V_3.

In the case of a diver the stationary frame of reference is the swimming pool.

Consider the following body with two axes of rotation, the vertical axis and the horizontal axis:

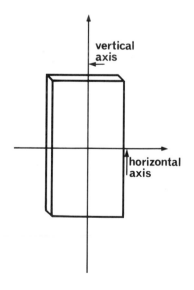

The total angular momentum L_t can be expressed as the sum of two component parts, one part L_v along the vertical axis and the other part L_h along the horizontal axis:

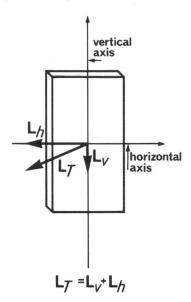

$$L_T = L_v + L_h$$

Now consider the body in a stationary frame of reference X-Y with its horizontal axis parallel to the X axis:

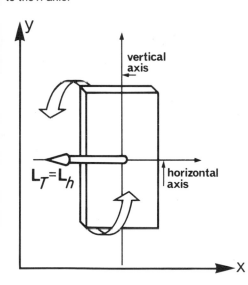

The body is spinning about the horizontal axis but has no twist about the vertical axis. Thus the total angular momentum L_t has a component L_h along the horizontal axis but no component L_v along the vertical axis. L_t therefore is equal to L_h. Note that the total angular momentum is parallel to the X axis. This situation corresponds to a diver who has left the board with spin but no twist. If the body is now tilted slightly over on its side, the total angular momentum L_t, by the law of conservation of angular momentum, will remain parallel to the X axis:

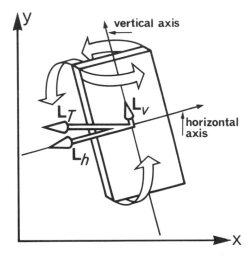

But now, when L_t is broken up into its two component parts, there is a component L_v along the vertical axis, and thus the body has developed a twist around the vertical axis.

Although L_v seems to be small, the twist will be fast because the radius of gyration around the vertical axis is now as small as possible.

A diver can tilt to the side by rotating his arms, initially stretched out to his sides, one above his head and the other down over his stomach. As his arms move in one direction, say clockwise, his body, because of the third law of Newton (action-reaction), will tilt in the other direction, counterclockwise.

If a diver tilts in this manner while he is spinning, he will develop a twist, and similarly, if he eliminates his tilt by reversing the action of his arms, he will stop the twist. Also, it is clear the amount of twist will be directly proportional to the amount of spin (angular momentum) started from the board.

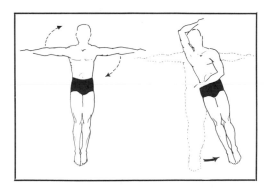